STARGATE
SG·1™
DIALING UP

Stargate SG-1
Dialing Up

ISBN: 9781848562325

Published by Titan Books
A division of Titan Publishing Group Ltd
144 Southwark St, London SE1 0UP

First edition August 2009
1 2 3 4 5 6 7 8 9 10

Visit our website: www.titanbooks.com

Did you enjoy this book? We love to hear from our readers. Please email us at readerfeedback@titanemail.com or write to us at Reader Feedback at the above address.

To receive advance information, news, competitions, and exclusive Titan offers online, please register as a member by clicking the "sign up" button on our website: www.titanbooks.com

A CIP catalogue record for this title is available from the British Library.

Printed and bound in China by C&C Offset Printing Co., Ltd.

STARGATE SG·1™

DIALING UP

THOMASINA GIBSON

Stargate SG-1 developed for television by
Brad Wright & Jonathan Glassner

TITAN BOOKS

Contents

Initiating the Cycle

"A gateway to the imagination has been opened and a new universe of action and adventure has been unleashed."
MGM statement, 1997

When *Stargate* the motion picture set the big screen alight in 1994, it also fired the imaginations of Jonathan Glassner and Brad Wright, who thought the idea of using an ancient portal to travel to a world far beyond our own intriguing to say the least. "I liked the original movie," admits Wright. "But I felt there was so much more to explore in terms of storytelling. For instance: what if the Stargate could be used to travel to many other places? What if we found the means to choose those destinations? What if we encountered other races and what might we learn from them?"

Jonathan Glassner takes up the story. "On a rainy Vancouver day in winter 1996, John Symes, the then president of MGM Worldwide Television, flew to the set of *The Outer Limits*, which I was executive producing at the time. He came to convince me to stay on the show for another season; I had been away from California for three years and wanted to go home. He asked me if there was anything else I wanted to do that would keep me up there. I told him that MGM had a movie in their library called *Stargate*, which I thought would make a great TV series and I would consider staying if I could create that show and produce it. His response was vague (for various legal, financial and political reasons, he wasn't sure he could do it). He went back to Los Angeles and I figured that was the end of that.

Above: A concept drawing for the early first season episode 'The Broca Divide'.

"Little did I know that John had posed the same question to Brad Wright (who was also working on *The Outer Limits*). And, independently of me, Brad had made the same request — he wanted to do *Stargate* for television.

"Cut to a month later. John Symes returns to Vancouver to meet with Brad and me. He called us into an office and said simply, 'How would you two feel about doing a *Stargate* series together?' Brad and I were thrilled by the idea. We both knew that it was going to be a huge undertaking and the thought of sharing the burden was appealing. Only one more issue remained — I told John that it must be understood up front that the show was going to be very expensive to produce. 'Not a problem, within reason,' he said. That's what John had been doing the past month — putting together a brilliant business plan involving two US networks, a large US station group, and huge international sales to pay for the show. He had already made it possible. Now all we had to do was make it a reality."

Having initiated the cycle, Symes set about persuading Richard Dean Anderson, a friend and colleague from

Above:
SG-1 on the lookout for trouble in 'Cold Lazarus'.

their days working together on *MacGyver*, to come on board. "John called me and said, 'I really want you to do this,'" recalls Anderson. "He sent me the tape so I watched the movie a few times, did my research and saw the potential of the movie as a great starting block for the series." The Jack O'Neill character also intrigued the actor: "He's a man trained to obey orders, but with the need to follow his own moral compass. I thought it would be interesting to draw out his humanity and sense of humour in situations where he's under pressure." Before embarking on his journey through the Stargate, Anderson made sure that everyone understood he would portray Colonel O'Neill his way, and inject the character with many of his own little foibles: "I have a very irreverent sense of humour. It's very dry, sarcastic, naughty, and I wanted to give O'Neill that kind of levity. Fortunately, they went along with me." *Stargate SG-1* afforded Anderson the chance to work with long-time business partner Michael Greenburg. "It had been some time since we'd worked on a television series together," Anderson remembers, "and we really wanted to do that. Thankfully, *Stargate* provided the perfect opportunity."

"What I liked about the idea, apart from working with Rick," agrees Greenburg, "was that here we had a science fiction premise that also had some basis in reality. Our Stargate Command, the SGC, is part of Space Command, which is an actual division of the United States Air Force. Our stories, in keeping with the mythology established in the movie, involve humans who were taken by alien invaders thousands of years ago and forced to act as slaves for, or 'hosts' to the Goa'uld." Greenburg feels much of *Stargate SG-1*'s huge success is down to the writers, who have managed to incorporate these factual, human and science fiction elements into a show in which "our universe is restricted only by the limit of our imaginations."

The job of creating this fertile universe in a practical sense fell to production designer Richard Hudolin. Describing his first meeting with Glassner and Wright, Hudolin recalls, "We got along very well personally and professionally; we just 'clicked'. There was no confusion as to where we were going. When you have designers and writers working together like that, everything is going to happen as it should. I started on my own almost straight away and worked for a couple of weeks to get the designs together for the pilot episode. I remember doing a presentation to a whole trailer-full of people, and they really bought into my designs for the Stargate Command sets."

At this point, Hudolin called in Thom Wells as construction co-ordinator and immediately hired an art department: "Basically a skeletal construction crew worked together with art director Bridget McGuire's 'magnificent seven' in the art department for around three weeks. We managed the shortest of breaks for Christmas 1996 before hiring 150 carpenters to just blast away at it to get the job done. It was an incredible push."

While this frenetic activity continued on set, a very laborious casting process was underway to find the other members of Jack O'Neill's team. Jonathan Glassner recalls the decision to cast Michael Shanks as Dr Daniel Jackson was far from easy. "We looked at around 500 men and finally narrowed it down to three that we thought were all very strong choices," he says. "We were torn, because all three actors had great strengths and they were all very different, but we just had a feeling, though we didn't even really see it in the audition, that Michael could do comedy. I think he was a little nervous at the audition, but we kept thinking, 'There's something about this guy. He's got a wit about him.' Then when shooting began, and the 'dailies' started coming in, we all went 'Thank God!'"

Above: Director Peter DeLuise tries to persuade RDA to read the script.

Shanks recalls that, even though none of them knew they would be cast at the time, there was an immediate bond between the actors who would become the SG-1 team: "We were sitting there at the audition, just talking away and going through the process, but there was something special between us. It was kind of funny, but great, walking on set the first day and seeing the same faces. It just felt right."

Brad Wright maintains he and Glassner were insistent from the start that Amanda Tapping was Samantha Carter: "We had a massive hunt for this cast but really, really wanted Amanda for the role." Their enthusiasm was not met with unanimous approval at first, but within five episodes, Tapping's determined portrayal of, as she puts it, "a scientist smack in the middle of an adventurous boys' club" received an overwhelming vote of confidence from all concerned. Glassner smiles, "We got a call saying, 'OK, guys, you were right. We would have been in trouble if we had cast anyone else in that part.'"

"Sam can hang with the men and do anything that's asked of her," Tapping says. "She's smart, determined, adventurous and definitely not afraid of a little excitement. I'm very similar to her in that way."

"When Christopher Judge walked in the room, before he said a word we went 'OK — that's him!'" laughs Wright. His co-executive producer adds, "I leaned over to Brad and whispered, 'Please, God, let him be able to act!' Then he read the part, did a great job and made Teal'c his own. We really lucked out with our cast."

Co-executive producer and writer Robert C. Cooper fondly remembers the first two seasons of the show as the time when quite a few risks were being taken: "We were finding our feet and exploring new avenues, and I'd say we got it right about fifty per cent of the time. We produced some of our best ever episodes during those seasons, but even our less than spectacular efforts provided valuable lessons for us to work on. It was an interesting rollercoaster of a ride for us, but by season three I feel we were almost there in terms of what would work best for the show."

SEASON ONE

REGULAR CAST:

Richard Dean Anderson (Colonel Jack O'Neill)

Michael Shanks (Dr Daniel Jackson)

Amanda Tapping (Captain Samantha Carter)

Christopher Judge (Teal'c)

Don S. Davis (General Hammond)

Children of the Gods

Apophis's Jaffa warriors arrive on Abydos.

When a group of hostile aliens emerges through an ancient transportation portal from the planet Abydos, Stargate Command sends Captain Jack O'Neill, two former colleagues and a new team member, astrophysicist Captain Samantha Carter, to investigate. Reunited with Dr Daniel Jackson, now married to local girl Sha're, and O'Neill's adopted son Skaara, the team are awed by Jackson's latest discovery: what appears to be a map of the Stargate system. When Skaara and Sha're are kidnapped, SG-1 must save the Abydans before General Hammond sends a nuclear weapon to destroy the planet.

Written by: Jonathan Glassner and Brad Wright
Directed by: Mario Azzopardi

Guest cast: Jay Acovone (Major Charles Kawalsky), Vaitiare Bandera (Sha're), Robert Wisden (Major Samuels), Peter Williams (Apophis), Brent Stait (Major Ferretti), Gary Jones (Technician), Alex Cruz (Skaara)

Hammond: "Have you thought about writing a book?"
O'Neill: "I've thought about it, but I'd have to shoot anybody that read it."

ONE OUTSTANDING MEMORY LINGERS in the minds of everyone involved in the filming of *Stargate SG-1*'s première episode, and that's "Rain!" "The first day of filming we had rain on a scale that was practically a national disaster," executive producer Brad Wright recalls, "talk about the wrath of the gods!"

"We had fifty extras all in intricate costumes," says make-up supervisor Jan Newman. "And we had prisoners all covered with dirt but, of course, it was meant to be dry dirt from a desert planet, not mud from a sodden British Columbia. Plus, we had Apophis and Teal'c covered in gold dust, which meant they had to be kept completely dry and away from any surface which might mar the sheen on their skin."

Peter Williams says that wearing Apophis's armour "wasn't so much flying by the seat of your pants as flying by the tip of your nose. I had two different versions of the head-dress: one made of rubber which weighed around sixty pounds, and one where the visor moved up and down which weighed much more. The pneumatic one was doubly uncomfortable because it was operated by a man standing off-camera, and the whole thing came and went within a centimetre of the tip of my nose. My frame of reference was the back of the helmet. If my head touched it, I'd be OK. If not — it was 'look out' time!"

The Enemy Within

Jackson and Carter try to prevent Kawalsky from going through the gate.

Written by:
Brad Wright
Directed by:
Dennis Berry

Guest cast:
Jay Acovone (Major Charles Kawalsky), Kevin McNulty (Dr Warner), Gary Jones (Technician), Alan Rachins (Colonel Kennedy), Warren Takeuchi (Young Doctor)

General Hammond refuses to approve the appointment of Teal'c to the team until military intelligence has "debriefed" the Jaffa. Whilst the suicidal forces of the Goa'uld continue to bombard the titanium alloy iris protecting the Stargate on Earth, O'Neill finds out that Kawalsky's headaches are caused by an unfriendly larva that has attached itself to his brain.

O'Neill (to Kawalsky): "If you don't make it — can I have your stereo?"

JAY ACOVONE WAS THRILLED but surprised when the call came to say he'd been offered the role of Kawalsky. "The casting director, Mary Jo Slater, called my agent and I went to the audition in the MGM building in Santa Monica," the actor remembers. "I did what I thought was a reasonably good job and went home. I figured that they'd be making a decision real soon, so when I didn't hear for a couple of weeks, I was disappointed, but put it down to experience and forgot about it. Then three weeks after I'd gone in, they called and said, 'We want you to play Kawalsky.' It was meant to be just one show — but I just keep popping up there." Asked if he had any thoughts on why his character got bumped off so early, the irrepressible Mr Acovone replies, "I was told that they wanted the guy who played him in the movie, but apparently he didn't want to do a series. They then said to him, 'How about if we kill Kawalsky off in the first show?' When I came on board, I told them I wanted to do a series very much, but the producers didn't have approval to do anything else, so I got killed off. That's my story and I'm sticking to it!"

Despite his demise, Kawalsky comes back to haunt his old friend O'Neill in 'The Gamekeeper' and in season three's 'Point of View'. Having "had a blast" in the episodes he's done so far, all the effervescent Mr Acovone really wants to ask the writers is, "When am I coming back again?" Executive producer Robert Cooper reassuringly replies, "No one ever dies in science fiction."

SG-1 travel to the planet Simarka and meet the Shavadai. Carter finds herself relegated to the role of second-class citizen in a community where it is death for a woman to even speak without permission from a man. Sam is further humiliated when the son of one chieftain tries to swap her for Nya, the daughter of an enemy. When the exchange is unsuccessful, Carter tries to arrange Nya's escape, only to face the girl's father in battle when the plans go awry.

Written by:
Katharyn Powers
Directed by:
Jeff Woolnough

Guest cast:
Cary-Hiroyuki Tagawa (Turghan), Jorge Vargas (Abu), Soon-Tek Oh (Moughal), Crystal Lo (Nya)

Sam (to Daniel): "Find me an anthropologist who dresses like this and I will eat this head-dress."

"I JUST REMEMBER THAT dress," shudders Amanda Tapping. Referring to the diaphanous blue affair which showed more than a suggestion of cleavage, she grins, "When the SG-1 guys and the crew saw it they all went 'Woo-hoo!' I just said, 'You know guys, smoke and mirrors. There's a lot of push me-pull you working here.' That's all it ever was and is all it's ever going to be!"

According to executive producer Jonathan Glassner, 'Emancipation' was one of the episodes shot "whilst we were still finding our feet" and which showed the way not to go as far as the Stargate universe was concerned: "It was too preachy. Science fiction is a very good medium for having little moral tales and subtle messages built into the stories, and that's what we were trying to do. We just went way too far; so we pulled back afterwards." Amanda Tapping concurs: "Because none of us really liked the episode, I was feeling a little off base with it. Although I did enjoy doing the fight sequence, especially working with the stunt co-ordinator for three days to get it right." Tapping laughs that the sequence was actually payback time for a certain member of the cast: "The Mongol warrior who ends up buying my character was very tough. He had my throat in a really tight grip and grabbed my hair right back, but then we had the fight sequence so I got my revenge."

The beautiful, technology-free planet Simarka.

THE BROCA DIVIDE

Carter and O'Neill, happy to be home.

Written by:
Jonathan Glassner
Directed by:
William Gereghty

Guest cast:
Teryl Rothery (Dr Janet Fraiser), Gary Jones (Technician), Gerard Plunkett (Councillor Tuplo), Danny Wattley (Johnson), Roxana Phillip (Melosha)

On planet P3X797, the SG-1 team discover a world with Bronze Age inhabitants on the light side of the globe; and a bunch of Neanderthals on the dark side. Returning through the Stargate, some of the team begin to display Neanderthal characteristics. Daniel and Teal'c discover they have been infected by a mysterious virus and they rush to find an antidote to the disease.

SG-3 Marine: "We'll watch your back side."
Daniel: "It's my front side I'm worried about."

"WHEN WE FIRST STARTED on the series, we were having a hard time trying to figure out the tone of the show. 'The Broca Divide' was one of our test shows," comments executive producer Jonathan Glassner. "The show was an attempt to have fun, and it's probably the closest to where we continued to go," he admits. He adds, "What was really great was how thrilled we were with Richard Dean Anderson," he enthuses. "I had no idea what he was capable of, apart from the straight man stuff he does so well. Richard did such a fantastic job, it made us start writing more things for him that were fun, and stretched him beyond what he's known for."

The episode also saw Teryl Rothery join the show. "Teryl played a big part in 'The Broca Divide'," says Glassner, "and, though Brad and I had worked with her many times before, that was the first time we saw the chemistry between her and the others — especially between her and Rick. That was the episode that made us decide to make her a little more of a regular."

The relationship between Dr Fraiser and O'Neill is what makes 'The Broca Divide' one of Teryl Rothery's favourite episodes. "There were so many great moments for Janet where she got to show her strength of character, the depth of her compassion for her patients and her dedication to the SG teams," the actress recalls. "But my favourite scenes have to be the ones with Richard Dean Anderson, especially the one where he asks Janet to experiment on him."

THE FIRST COMMANDMENT

The commanding officer of SG-9 is terrorising the people of a distant planet into believing he is a god. Captain Jonas Hanson demands the primitive cave dwellers rebuild the giant Goa'uld temples in his honour. Daniel Jackson and Teal'c set out to convince the people of the planet that Hanson's power is man-made rather than divine, and that they can build their own future without the need for false gods.

Written by:
Robert C. Cooper
Directed by:
Dennis Berry

Guest cast:
William Russ (Captain Jonas Hansen), Roger R. Cross (Lieutenant Connor), Zahf Hajee (Jamala), Adrian Hughes (Lieutenant Baker), D. Neil Mark (Frakes)

Daniel: "This tastes like chicken."
Sam: "What's wrong with that?"
Daniel: "It's macaroni cheese."

BRAD WRIGHT ADMITS THE creative team were not completely happy with this episode, "This story is not a fan favourite," he says. "It was a great idea, but not for one of the first six *Stargates*. In retrospect, it didn't make sense that a guy could have a 'God' complex so early in the programme and would they have picked a candidate so poorly? It's one of those where we have to admit we'd bitten off more than we could chew. On the other hand, it was a major learning experience, and made us capable of making *Stargate SG-1* much better."

Robert C. Cooper confesses that it's his least favourite episode in season one: "Even though the story idea got me the job on *Stargate*, I feel there were better choices that could have been made." On reflection, Cooper thinks the idea of a past romance having a bearing on how Carter would conduct herself in the field wasn't right for the character at that time. "I got a lot of feedback about that one," he smiles.

"It was the first cheery moment that I got to play," says Amanda Tapping. "I hit the guy and say, 'Well, that was refreshing.' Though when I did it, my gun swung round and whacked me on the hip and I'm like, 'Wow! That hurts.' So it was kind of like karma. I hit someone, so I got hit back."

O'Neill goes undercover.

Cold Lazarus

Close encounters with a crystal on P3X562.

Written by:
Jeffery F. King
Directed by:
Kenneth J. Girotti

Guest cast:
Teryl Rothery (Dr Fraiser), Harley Jane Kozak (Sara O'Neill), Gary Jones (Technician), Wally Dalton (Sara's Father), Kyle Graham (Charlie O'Neill)

A being from P3X562 duplicates O'Neill and returns through the Stargate in his stead. The doppelgänger seeks out O'Neill's wife, Sara, in an effort to find his son Charlie. Meanwhile, Sam and Daniel realise that the beings cannot survive in the Earth's intense electromagnetic field, and therefore the O'Neill double could self-destruct.

Teal'c: "Your world is strange."
Daniel: "So's yours."

ALTHOUGH IT MAY HAVE looked as though the startlingly bright alien landscape of P3X562 was the result of some super visual effects, executive producer Michael Greenburg reveals that 'Cold Lazarus' was actually filmed in a sulphur pit. "We supplemented the colour with some matte painting," he explains. Laughing about sulphur's particularly noxious odour, he insists, "It didn't smell that bad. It's just that it was a very hot day, and the combination of the terrain, the heat and the substance itself made life a bit of a challenge."

Greenburg also remembers this episode being an emotional one: "Rick was really into it, because it went into O'Neill's relationship with his son, and so it was always going to be emotional and very dramatic. Fortunately, it's a pretty light-hearted set and the director was a jokester, so he kept us going."

"There have been many wonderful episodes," says Hank Cohen, the current president of MGM Television, "but 'Cold Lazarus' is the one that sticks in my memory. I remember when we took it to MIPCOM [an annual event to showcase new productions and concepts in television and film]. We were showing it to buyers from the UK and Germany. I stepped out of the room for a moment — I'd already seen it eight million times — and when I came back five people in the room were in tears. I knew then that not only did we have a show that would appeal to 'slaves' to the sci-fi genre, but the humanity of our stories would appeal to anyone."

The Nox

Daniel encounters the Nox.

Whilst on a trip to seek out some creatures known as Fenri, who Teal'c remembers as having the power of invisibility, the SG-1 team get into a skirmish with a Goa'uld hunting party and are killed. Fortunately, a mystical group of fairy-like beings are on hand to weave their magic and revive the group. Amazed by their healing powers but concerned that their peaceful demeanour will attract more unwelcome attention from the Goa'uld, SG-1 offer US military might to defend the apparently defenceless little beings. The Nox once more surprise the team by revealing that they have their own solution to any attack.

Written by:
Hart Hanson
Directed by:
Charles Correll

Guest cast:
Peter Williams (Apophis), Armin Shimerman (Anteaus), Ray Xifo (Ohper), Gary Jones (Technician), Frida Betrani (Lya), Terry David Mulligan (Secretary of Defense David Swift), Addison Ridge (Nafrayu), Michasa Armstrong (Shak'l)

O'Neill: "The very young do not always do as they are told."

CHRISTOPHER JUDGE CONSIDERS THE place where the Nox dwell as one of his favourite planets. "If I had the choice, I would definitely visit the place where the Nox live," he says. "They are special. In their gentle, positive way they taught us to ask: 'Who are we, in our egocentric way, to say how someone else should live or conduct their lives?' I thought that without beating everyone over the head with it, it was a great learning episode."

Colleague Michael Shanks feels there was another aspect to their learning experience: "Armin Shimerman was very much the mentor in more ways than one. Having been part of a long-running science fiction franchise [as Quark in *Star Trek: Deep Space Nine*], he had more experience than any of us in working through the various practical challenges this medium throws at you. He understood what we were trying to do in terms of building the mythology and quietly shared that experience with us. It was wonderful working with him."

It wasn't just sweetness and light on set that week. "I remember this episode significantly for one particular line," jokes Apophis's alter ego, the very benign Peter Williams. "It's directed towards Jack O'Neill and I yell, 'Fool! I will kill you!' Kind of ironic considering what happens a little later on in the series, but I particularly enjoyed delivering that line."

Colonel Jack O'Neill

O'Neill: "Next time I want to help someone, feel free to give a swift kick."

Talking with Richard Dean Anderson on set in Vancouver, it's hard to distinguish where the actor ends and Colonel Jack O'Neill begins, because they're men with a very similar take on life. Open, straight-forward, charming and disarming, both men have a special job to do, don't deviate from their task and yet manage to inject a distinct sense of levity into the proceedings. "We try not to take ourselves too seriously," he smiles. "We do explore some contentious issues on the show, and often investigate the more serious of life's aspects, but we try to keep a lightness and a sense of humour about the whole approach."

Asked why he decided to take on the dual roles of executive producer and leading actor in the series, the ex-*MacGyver* star shrugs, "Because I hadn't. Done a science fiction show that is. I'd always said I'd try anything once, and when this opportunity presented itself it seemed the right time for a foray into the realms of science fiction."

Stargate SG-1's première episode sees O'Neill dragged out of voluntary retirement to head up a motley crew of experts, including an anthropologist, an astrophysicist and a chap from a galaxy far, far away. The first defence against a hoard of marauding predators, the newly-formed unit proceed to regularly throw themselves through a watery portal in order to seek out new worlds and civilisations, in the hope that someone, somewhere will share the technology and knowledge needed to defeat the Goa'uld.

"When I looked at the film I liked the character of O'Neil [played by Kurt Russell], but knew I'd have to do things differently," Anderson recalls of his approach to the role. So, as well as a slight difference in the spelling of his name (a fact touched on in the second season's 'Secrets', when Anderson's character quips, "There is another Colonel O'Neil, who spells his name with one 'l'") the characters couldn't be more dissimilar. There's still an initial animosity between the key players in the series, for example O'Neill makes it clear in 'Children of the Gods' that he has "a problem with scientists". He thinks the anthropologist in his team is a geek (Daniel Jackson notes this in his diary in 'Fire and Water'), and he gets 'weirded out' by Teal'c, as evidenced by an off-the-cuff remark made during 'Need'. However, the Colonel's leadership skills, such as they are — "I think this is supposed to be where I say something profound — nothing comes to mind. Let's go!" he says in 'Within the Serpent's Grasp' — and obvious concern for his 'kids', brings the team together.

A consummate action man, Richard Dean Anderson's road to *Stargate SG-1* has thrown a few energetic

challenges in his path. Having set his heart on becoming a professional hockey player (a dream shared by colleague Michael Shanks), Anderson had to abandon that ambition when he broke both his arms. Undaunted, he embarked on an epic bike ride across North America. En route he fought forest fires in British Columbia, a role he claims as one of his most rewarding to date, and also worked as a whale trainer in California. He enjoyed some wild times as a DJ whilst at college in Ohio, and sparkled as a jester-singer-mime-juggler in a sixteenth century Renaissance-style cabaret in Los Angeles. All stuff that should come in pretty handy when it's time to entertain the true love of his life — his daughter Wylie.

For a man who seems to flit from experience to experience, Anderson exhibits extreme staying power when it comes to television shows. Cast as Dr Jeff Webber in *General Hospital*, he continued in the role of American daytime TV's medical heartthrob for five years. He then became the focus of international attention when his even longer run as *MacGyver* went into worldwide syndication. The part called for Anderson to play "an intellectual-type adventurer — a kind of Indiana Jones. Henry Winkler was the co-producer on the show. He told me I got the part as soon as I put my glasses on to read the script."

Although he admits that after the seven-year stint on *MacGyver* "everyone was getting a little tired and ready to move on to the next challenge", Anderson went on to make two highly successful *MacGyver* films with business partner Michael Greenburg. The two also executive produced the critically acclaimed series *Legend*. With tongue firmly in cheek Anderson warns, "Don't get me started on *Legend*. It was one of the best projects I've ever been involved in and damn it, I'm a little bitter that it didn't continue." The show was an entertaining piece of nonsense about a journalist with a fantastic alter ego. Given that the subject matter would endear it to media types all over the world, this particular journalist agrees *Legend*'s demise is a crying shame. Luckily, *Stargate SG-1* was just around the corner to take Anderson's mind off it.

As for Jack O'Neill's life journey to Stargate Command — that's a story best left to the man himself...

MEMO FROM COLONEL O'NEILL

By RICHARD DEAN ANDERSON

I'll just start where it gets interesting for me. The kid stuff, in retrospect, seems normal by any objective perspective: mom and dad divorced, sibling rivalry brought forth a myriad of bloody confrontations (to date I can claim seventy-three stitches), school was a distraction, dogs were always my best friends, and to this day I don't trust cats.

My grandfather was an ore miner in northern Minnesota and then became a banker, toiling under the truly evil eyes of a manager bent on demeaning the lowly likes of gentle men. Eventually gramps ran for and was elected mayor of his hometown. Nana had the patience of a statue, the mind of an educated diplomat, and the beauty of an Irish/Scandinavian doll. She kept gramps in line. They both drank, but his social interaction always seemed to push the lines of propriety after a few, and she would have to tether him in... A well-intentioned reminder of who was in charge.

My dad is a great guy and made some unique contributions to my development. He flew big planes in WWII, dropping paratroopers on D-Day, making loops between England and France for two tours. I still grill him for stories. My mom is a computer genius and a Life Master bridge player. She also paints, weaves and sculpts with glorious, artistic panache. But it was my dad's brother, Uncle Fred, who kick-started my interest in flight. He never saw combat action, but he flew jets – and I love jets.

The seed was sown. Off I went. Zipped through all the preliminaries of flight training, cut a swath to Top Gun, eventually found a home with Special Forces. It all came together in Special Forces – a sweet niche of naughty doings. Spent some time training the Norwegian SF contingent, with a sharp focus on mountain survival and commando tactics. It was fun, and I still stay in touch with a half dozen equally frostbitten individuals.

I can't talk about what I do these days professionally, but I spend a lot of time in Northern Minnesota, soaking up the spirit of my granddad, and sniffing the pine-permeated air. I go fishing, but to this day, I have never caught one.

General Ryan to Hammond: "Looks like you've got yourself a bit of a handful there, George."

As anyone from an airforce chief of staff to an Asgard will testify, Colonel Jack O'Neill is a force to be reckoned with. Not just because of his natural ability in combat in the field, but also his sharp wit, which lies in wait to ambush any unsuspecting victim. In 'Into the Fire' when the vengeful Hathor waves a voracious symbiote in his face in an attempt to invoke some fear, O'Neill quips, "What? The grey doesn't bother you?" No wonder the poor old Queen stormed off in a huff. "I like to incorporate the mischievous elements of my personality with those of Jack O'Neill," confesses Richard Dean Anderson. "It was one of the things I insisted be allowed to happen before I signed on for this job, and I continue to try to get away with as much as I possibly can." Ask any of the other members of the cast and crew and everyone will come up with a shining example of his irreverent approach to life and *Stargate SG-1*. "We do have to put up with a lot of Homer Simpson-isms from Rick," sighs Amanda Tapping. "If any of us fluffs a line or the director suggests some minor change Rick will automatically go 'D'oh!' He makes me smile every time he does it."

Anderson injects more than just his sense of humour into his portrayal of Colonel O'Neill. Some of the practical skills he's learnt along life's path have come in handy every now and then. 'Window of Opportunity' gave him the chance to show off his talent for juggling. "I learned how to juggle when I moved to California, had no money whatsoever and was living in a shack in the backyard of some people's house," he grins.

On a more serious note, Anderson is happy to offer his personal opinion or take on a particular story slant. One that he recalls in particular is the storyline of season three's 'A Hundred Days'. "In [that episode] I don't think O'Neill would ever have left Laira if he knew she was pregnant. In fact, if we ever did revisit that story and it turns out O'Neill did father a child, then I'd like to see him with a daughter. That preference is for no reason other than that he's already had a son, and it would be interesting to see how his relationship with a daughter would unfold."

O'Neill: "We've stayed ahead of the game only because we didn't bite off more than we could chew... normally."

Reflecting on what his character has endured over the seasons Anderson comments: "I suppose the Colonel has had quite a time. Remind me what happened again?" In common with his fictional *Stargate* counterpart, the actor can suffer from selective memory loss, which seems to worsen when asked to recount some details from the show. "Can't I tell you about my new bike?" he asks. "Or what about my random thoughts I'm thinking of publishing — as if anyone will read them." Assurances that at least one poor soul would eagerly pore over his collected ramblings accompany a stern admonishment that there must be one or two incidents that stick in his notoriously vague mind. "What?" he insists. "Here, have a look at these pictures of my daughter."

Despite his apparent amnesia, the actor offers a few opinions on the way *Stargate SG-1* has progressed. "Obviously, Michael Shanks's departure at the end of season five signalled a time of transition for us all. Michael had expressed some concerns about his involvement — or his perceived lack of it — in the show, and indicated that he wanted to move on. Michael has always been a very valued member of our group, so the wheels were put in motion to accommodate his wishes. He knew that he could return at any time, and in fact has done so several times throughout our sixth season. He is a very solid actor. He's also flexible enough to deal with my bursts of spontaneity, so I always have good moments with him."

Brief Candle

Story by:
Steven Barnes
Teleplay by:
Katharyn Powers
Directed by:
Mario Azzopardi

Guest cast:
Teryl Rothery (Dr Fraiser), Bobbie Phillips (Kynthia), Harrison Coe (Alekos), Gabrielle Miller (Thetys), Gary Jones (Technician)

Daniel Jackson delivers a baby moments after SG-1 set foot on the planet Argos, and is invited to celebrate the birth. The team encounters a joyful community who party during the day, but collapse once the sun sets. Drugged and seduced, O'Neill wakes to find that he is showing signs of rapid ageing. The team learn that the Argosians' lifespan is only one hundred days, though O'Neill is ageing even faster than that. The team must find a cure before his time runs out.

O'Neill: "I was kinda looking forward to a little shuffle-board with the fellas."

MAKE-UP SUPERVISOR JAN NEWMAN declares 'Brief Candle' one of her most satisfying projects. "The characters were aged from forty-five to a hundred years old in seven stages," she explains. "The first three stages were achieved using only paint. For the final four stages, prosthetic appliances were added. Jayne Dancose and Dave DuPuis were the special prosthetic visual effect artists and did an amazing job." Newman adds, "One of the things that fascinates me about the ageing process is the way in which people's eyes change. It was very important to me that Richard Dean Anderson's eyes aged the way they should, and I was delighted when the lens technicians came up with a pair of contact lenses that really finished the job."

Newman worried it would be difficult getting the actor to stay put to apply the make-up. "Usually I can only pin Richard down for around seven minutes," she laughs, "but he was so intrigued by the old age procedure that it was fine. Taking the prosthetics off was the worst part. It took around two hours per day, and by that time he really was getting antsy!"

As on-set producer, Michael Greenburg acknowledges Anderson's professionalism during the filming: "It was very hard for Rick because of that make-up. He was being prepared for camera for anything between four and six hours every day. But I also respect him for his incredible performance — from the piping voice to the stoop and shuffle. He did a wonderful job."

Daniel and Teal'c observe the citizens of the planet Argos.

Thor's Hammer

The murderous Unas.

On a peaceful mission to establish friendly relations with the people of Cimmeria, Teal'c and O'Neill are trapped by a mysterious bolt from the blue. They are transported to a strange underground labyrinth, from whence they must escape not only the caves but also the clutches of a very hungry, murderous creature called an Unas. In order to find and rescue their friends, Sam and Daniel must enlist the help of Kendra, a former Goa'uld host who escaped the labyrinth years before.

Written by:
Katharyn Powers
Directed by:
Brad Turner

Guest cast:
Gaylyn Gorg (Kendra), Vincent Hammond (Unas), Tamsin Kelsey (Gairwyn), Mark Gibbon (Thor), James Earl Jones (the Voice of Unas)

O'Neill (about Thor's hologram): "I think we just got the answering machine."

"EPISODES LIKE THIS ONE are difficult to pull off and make 'real', for want of a better word in sci-fi," Michael Greenburg admits, "because ultimately it's actors in suits. Fortunately, we found the very best special make-up effects people to help us." Speaking particularly of the Unas creature, Greenburg says, "Steve Johnson in LA is a real pro at making these alien suits look great. The way he applies the prosthetics really utilises the expressions of the actors. Remarkably, their skills shine through the rubber. Usually all you get is 'eyes', but with Steve doing the suits and prosthetics, you get the acting talents of the performers coming through."

Producer John Smith remembers being incredibly impressed by the talents of the prosthetic artist and cast: "They had a few problems getting it just right, but all credit to them for the great job they did." Although the Unas creature looks horrifying, Michael Greenburg reveals that all is not quite as it appears. "Since we made 'Thor's Hammer' we've been to the planet where they were conceived," he points out, "and met the Unas prior to their being taken over by the snakes. The Unas are actually good beings, very warm and friendly. They just look a little scary."

"You know," adds Greenburg, "when we destroyed the Goa'uld trap to allow Teal'c to escape, we literally left the door open for the Goa'uld to come back and haunt us. Which is exactly what happens much further along the way."

The Torment of Tantalus

Jackson discovers the secrets of Ernest's remarkable room.

Written by:
Robert C. Cooper
Directed by:
Jonathan Glassner

Guest cast:
Elizabeth Hoffman (Catherine Langford), Keene Curtis (Ernest Littlefield), Gary Jones (Technician), Duncan Fraser (Professor Langford), Nancy McClure (Young Catherine), Paul McGillion (Young Ernest)

Daniel Jackson discovers that in 1945 a young professor, Ernest Littlefield, travelled through the wormhole, and was left stranded. SG-1 find the professor, and discover a room that holds the combined wisdom of four alien civilisations. The group must try to repair the damaged dial home device before the structure they are in disintegrates.

Daniel: "The Pentagon said this was everything."
Jack: "Oh Please! The Pentagon's lost entire countries."

"THERE WERE SOME TRULY major visual effects created for this episode," recalls producer John Smith. "They had the big castle, the big hole and the chamber with all the 'meaning of life' stuff. It looked fantastic." One of the most amusing aspects for Smith was the way in which the cast and crew pulled together when the director suffered a minor memory slip. "This is probably slanderous and I apologise Mario," he grins, "but Mario Azzopardi simply forgot what he was meant to be filming. He looked at the call sheet and realised we had everybody there ready to shoot, but he hadn't had time to prepare. Being the genius he is, he just prepped it then and there, and pulled off some of the best scenes in the entire series. That's the nature of his talent."

"The floating doodads (very technical term) which made up 'the meaning of life stuff' in Ernest's chamber was a really good job," comments visual effects supervisor James Tichenor. "It was done with John Gajdecki and North West Imaging. Most language is written on paper or in stone, so we wanted to represent some ideas in 3D. The tricky thing was getting a sense of depth, while still making sure the symbols were readable in such a big space. When you make things that were further away appear a little clearer it kind of wrecks the depth. It was like two steps forward and one step back for us, because everything we did to make it easier to read the symbols actually worked against us in the shot. Still, it was a very pretty set!"

BLOODLINES

Teal'c returns to his home planet of Chulak in order to prevent his son Rya'c from becoming host to an infant Goa'uld, and thus a slave to Apophis. Aided by Bra'tac, Teal'c's 130 year-old Jaffa mentor, the team arrive in time to stop the implantation ceremony. However, Teal'c's wife is livid after he disrupts proceedings, killing the larva which would have saved his ailing child's life. Prepared to make the ultimate sacrifice by giving up his own larva to save his son, the Jaffa is restored when Sam and Daniel arrive bearing an unexpected gift.

Story by:
Mark Saraceni
Teleplay by:
Jeff King
Directed by:
Mario Azzopardi

Guest cast:
Tony Amendola (Bra'tac), Teryl Rothery (Dr Fraiser), Salli Richardson (Drey-Auc), Neil Denis (Rya'c)

O'Neill (to Bra'tac): "Hey! Hey! Hey! Who are you calling a hassock?"

"'BLOODLINES' IS ONE OF my all time favourites because we gain some insight into Teal'c's deeper, more vulnerable side," begins Christopher Judge. "Until then, we mostly see him as a person who doesn't show much emotion. It's not that Teal'c's not emotional. It's that he has so much emotion that if everything that's boiling on the inside was to bubble to the surface, he would lose control. I have three kids of my own, so I could really relate to the character's dilemma of having returned to resolve some personal issues with his wife and son, only to leave them once more. It was a great episode for me as we get to meet Teal'c's mentor Bra'tac and get an idea of where Teal'c gets his strength of will and character, and what it means to be a Jaffa warrior."

Judge also feels much of the passion behind the Jaffa's actions is hinted at in 'Bloodlines'. "His objective in the episode is to prevent his son from becoming a slave to Apophis, but it also indicates that Teal'c's super-objective is to free all Jaffa from the slavery of the Goa'ulds. I see the likes of Bra'tac and Teal'c as the civil rights leaders of their time. In spite of the great sacrifice he has to make, Teal'c takes the chance to be free, and to free his people from the oppressors. From what I've gathered when speaking to guys who watch the show, most people see him the same way as I do, which is heroic and noble."

Teal'c returns home.

FIRE AND WATER

Daniel and Nem forging a friendship.

Story by: Brad Wright
Teleplay by: Katharyn Powers
Directed by: Allan Eastman

Guest cast: Gerard Plunkett (Nem), Teryl Rothery (Dr Fraiser), Gary Jones (Technician)

SG-1 return from the planet Oannes without Daniel, who they last saw being engulfed in flames. But Jackson is being held prisoner by Nem, an amphibious being, who wants to find Omoroca – who lived on Earth 4,000 years ago. Daniel agrees to a potentially life-threatening brain scan. Disturbed by dreams that Daniel is still alive, the team ultimately return to Oannes to find answers.

Daniel: "I would rather die than stay here in the knowledge that I would never see my wife or my friends again."

"THE THING I LOVED most was that 'Fire and Water' had an entire emotional arc going on for me," says Michael Shanks. "Opportunities like that are few and far between in *Stargate* because it's mostly about our reactions to what we see, rather than what we're put through. This was one of the strongest experiences I had within the first season. I remember thinking that, actor-wise, you take a huge risk when you do that kind of episode. You put yourself right 'out there'. It's potentially very embarrassing to go in and say to some guy in a rubber suit, 'What are we talking about and what are you emoting about?' It's so crazily fictitious."

Speaking of his performance Shanks says, "I was young and naïve, and I think eager enough to completely throw myself into it, and commit to the wackiness entirely. Fortunately Gerard Plunkett, who played Nem, was great and did so much through that suit. He's a fine, strong actor and the director Allan Eastman was also great to work with. He gave us free rein to do whatever we wanted. He only directed one episode of *Stargate* but his was my favourite director's cut. Considering it was one of those shows that looked quite 'iffy' on the page, it turned out rather well."

"This was another risky episode," Brad Wright confirms. "I knew Michael Shanks could deliver in this difficult role, but every time you put your antagonist in a rubber suit, you'd better hope the actor pulls it off. I thought Gerard Plunkett did a tremendous job."

HATHOR

Daniel comes under the influence of Hathor.

Super-bitch Hathor – a Goa'uld who has taken on the persona of an Egyptian goddess – awakes from a 2,000 year slumber and kills the archaeologists who disturbed her. She then inveigles her way into the Stargate facility and seduces all the men on the base, convincing them to assist in her plan for world domination. It's up to Carter and the other women on the base to fight back.

Story by: David Bennett, Carren & J. Larry Carroll
Teleplay by: Jonathan Glassner
Directed by: Brad Turner

Guest cast: Teryl Rothery (Dr Fraiser), Suanne Braun (Hathor), Dave Hurtubise (Dr Kleinhouse), Amanda O'Leary (Dr Cole)

Daniel: "Hathor was the Egyptian goddess of fertility, inebriety and music."
Jack: "Sex, drugs, and rock and roll?"
Daniel: "In a manner of speaking."

"I SAW ON TV that an archaeologist had found an intact crypt in Egypt," reveals Jonathan Glassner. "I thought, 'God, what if a Goa'uld was still trapped inside a tomb?' According to ancient mythology, Ra married his mother. So, I spun it off from there and, yes, she really was the goddess of sex, drugs, and rock and roll! In fact, the black widow legend is based loosely on her because she killed most of the men she had sex with. She was a nasty, nasty woman."

Whilst, according to Glassner, Suanne Braun, the South African actress who portrays Hathor, was a delight, filming one of her scenes was less so: "You know where she is in the big bath tub and all those little baby Goa'ulds are supposed to be coming out of her? Well, we were in hell! We could not get that scene to work. We had near on 1,000 of those little latex wormy things and we dumped them into the tub, thinking that the churning water would make them slime all around her. Instead they just floated to the top and sat there with the water churning away underneath. Then the visual effects guys, gods that they are, said, 'Hey, you want us to fix that for ya?' They cut out each of those stupid little rubber things in post production and computer-animated them! So it's all down to those guys that we got the little critters jumping in and out of the water."

Jonathan Glassner: "Without a doubt, we have some of the best make-up artists in North America on our team."

Jan Newman initially took on the role of make-up supervisor on *Stargate SG-1* with some reluctance. "I had been working on features mostly and didn't want to do episodic work for a while. However, when it transpired that Richard Dean Anderson and Michael Greenburg [who she had got to know on *MacGyver*] had specifically asked for me, I couldn't turn it down. I would crawl over broken glass for them." First, she rented a copy of the movie because "I wanted to create a look specially for *Stargate SG-1*, but needed to get a 'feel' of what had been done previously." But there was still a surprise to come for Newman and her team. "When we signed on we thought it was all going to be pretty straightforward, but when we turned up for the pilot... There was a multitude of extra cast members and they were far from ordinary. We had aliens in the most fabulous costumes, so we designed special eye make-up to enhance the effect."

For Newman, the collaboration between the art directors, costume and special prosthetic make-up artists to create the helmet structure for Apophis and his Jaffa was particularly pleasing. "Moulds were taken of the actors' heads so that the capped helmets would fit snugly. Then they were made to resemble impenetrable armour and given this wonderful sheen. It was all a major pain in the backside to recreate that for each individual at the time, but to see them all marching along together was truly amazing."

Above: An aged O'Neill in 'Brief Candle'.

Opposite page: Teal'c's boils and blisters in 'Bane'.

Newman's crew's initial solution for creating the distinctive forehead mark of Apophis's serpent guard was a rubber stamp, "but it didn't work because everyone's forehead is different. So then we tried to stencil it on by cutting out the design and adding tattoo colour." Thankfully, technological advancements soon made the process far easier and quicker. "The art department creates the design on computer and produces a peel-off vinyl transfer which we stick on and then cover with silicone based paint. Now the tattoo stays on all day even with the vagaries of our Vancouver weather."

Stargate SG-1's normally patient make-up supremo does admit to one particularly challenging aspect of her job, but it also makes her laugh every day. "Christopher Judge!" she grins. "He has such a rambunctious nature that it's a challenge keeping his make-up in place. If he jumps into a vehicle or ducks into a trailer on set; to simply brush his head on the doorframe means we have to re-create his look. He's very high maintenance, but utterly charming with it." Still, Newman is grateful that Teal'c's make-up isn't more complex. "Originally, Teal'c was supposed to look

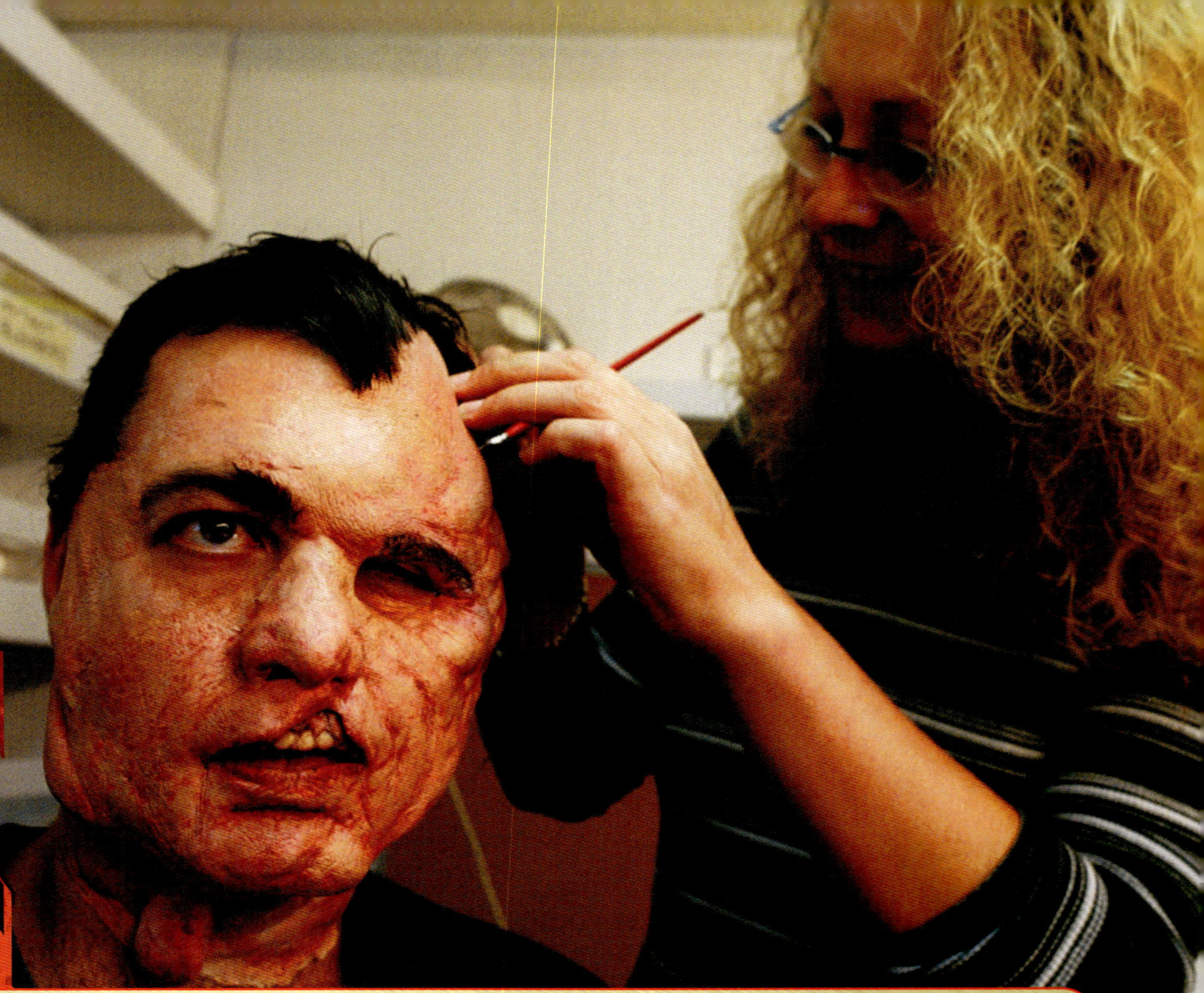

Above: Finishing Nirrti's evil handiwork.

Below left: The elegantly coiffured Amanda Tapping.

Below right: A battered and bruised Teal'c.

Brad Wright: "Our make-up department produces phenomenal results on a day-to-day basis. They truly deserve every Gemini nomination they've received."

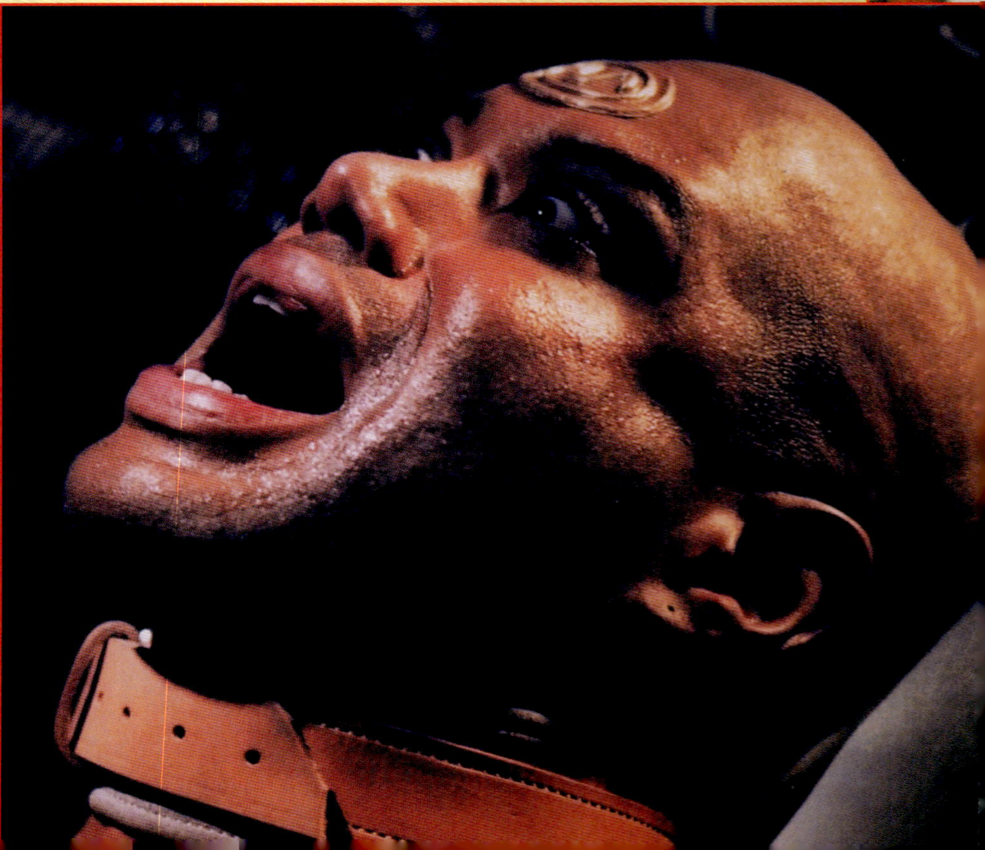

more like the stylised version of an Egyptian. He started out with long, droopy, prosthetic ears and had a long, braided beard like the depictions of the Pharaohs. He would have looked spectacular and it was a wonderful concept, but when I saw it I just groaned, because I thought about how difficult it would be to keep that look on a day-to-day, minute-to-minute basis." Newman says Wright's and Glassner's decision to go with the present look was "one of the best they made."

If Teal'c is high maintenance, Jack O'Neill is high speed. "The biggest thing with Richard Dean Anderson is getting him to sit still long enough for us to get him ready for camera!" Newman laughs. "He has a very short attention span, and all he wants to do is come in, get it done and move on to the rest of his day."

When pushed for particular make-up favourites, Jan says that for her and her assistants Margaret and Christopher, "Richard's Neanderthal look in 'The Broca Divide' and old-age make-up from 'Brief Candle' are the ones we talk about most."

HAIR TODAY...

By Key Hairdresser PATRICK O'BRIEN

My work day usually starts at approximately 6am, although there are days when I start at the unearthly hour of 4.30am. It all depends on the number of main and extra cast members we have on the day's call sheet, and the time of 'set call', which is when the camera should start rolling for the day's filming. I like to get to the unit at least half an hour before my call time, so I can get my breakfast – a very important start to my day!

The next thing I do is read the parts of the script that are being shot that day, and check with my script breakdown to see if any hair changes are necessary. If some of the day's filming involves a continuation of something we started at an earlier date, I refer to the continuity photos taken at the time we filmed that portion, so I can match the look.

The continuity photos are vital. They're kept in albums, and carefully labelled to indicate which episode they're from. We also use the photos when it comes to getting our recurring characters ready for the camera. There are quite a few characters that return every season, and some will return more than a couple of times within a year. Occasionally a character will return after many years away, for example appearing briefly in the first season, and then coming back in the fifth. In this case I have to go right back to the first season's album, and find the picture of that character. Sometimes the role will be taken by a different person, as in the case of Teal'c's wife, so revising the photos is essential. Taking into account that time has passed (and in the case of Teal'c's wife, her life had been very hard since Teal'c left Abydos), the photos are invaluable to help me get as close as possible to how they would look now.

Although we do still use Polaroid cameras in some instances, I take continuity photos with a digital camera these days, and have a lap top computer with a printer, so I can print the previous day's photos in the morning. I find the digital camera gives a more detailed photo than a Polaroid.

Depending on who is in the first scene to be shot that day, we prepare them for camera in priority of appearance. Richard Dean Anderson will occasionally come in and wash his hair at the basin; sometimes he will need a shave, which could be with an electric razor, or a wet shave. Many times he will actually need to look a mess, because the script calls for O'Neill to be in a state of distress, depending on what challenge SG-1 are up against that day. I usually cut his hair at the start of an episode.

Amanda Tapping has her hair cut short of late. She has wonderful bone structure and lovely big eyes, which the shorter hair shows off to a decidedly flattering advantage. Christopher Judge shaves his head for the part, so there's not a lot of styling required there! I clipper cut Don Davis's hair very short, military style, in keeping with his role as General Hammond.

As well as styling our main actors, my assistant Rose and I also see to it that the additional cast members (as many as twenty to twenty-five at times) are suitably styled for their roles as guest stars and background players. Our job then is to maintain the look throughout the day, and make any changes needed to keep the continuity, also keeping an eye on any script changes (which happen on a daily basis). We often film out of the studio in very heavy rain or sweltering heat, so keeping our actors comfortable and maintaining the look is quite a task! Thankfully, our cast is very easy going and loves to laugh and have fun, so the frequent twelve to fourteen hour days pass with very little stress at all.

SINGULARITY

O'Neill and Teal'c make a break for the Gate.

Written by:
Robert C. Cooper
Directed by:
Mario Azzopardi

Guest cast:
Teryl Rothery (Dr Fraiser), Katie Stuart (Cassandra), Gary Jones (Technician), Kevin McNulty (Dr Warner)

When SG-1 visit planet P8X987 they find that the whole population has been wiped out by a strange disease – except for one little girl. A deep bond develops between Carter and the child, Cassandra, but it is discovered that a metallic device growing inside the girl is actually a time bomb, set by the Goa'uld in an effort to destroy Earth.

Carter: "You didn't think the Colonel had a telescope on his roof just to look at the neighbours, did you?"

AMANDA TAPPING RETAINS SPECIAL memories of some very touching moments during filming. "During the crying scene in the elevator, the crew were just so silent," she remembers. "That day at lunch someone stood and said, 'Let's take grace' and we did. I was really touched."

Peter DeLuise attests, "Mario Azzopardi, the director, is a very passionate, volatile Maltese man and when Carter leaves Cassandra, it's obvious that she's very moved, particularly when she's kicking the crap out of the lift — you can see Mario's passion come through."

"The director kept saying, 'OK, do it again. I need more'," Tapping agrees, "but I was bawling my eyes out already. I was in the darkest place, and, finally, on the last take, with the cameras rolling he said, 'Amanda, you have left this little girl in this horrible place and you are an evil person.' I just thought, 'I don't need this, I've already got it figured out,' so I turned and yelled, 'Shut up! Get out of here!' And he said, 'Good! Now we shoot!' Afterwards he said, 'Hey, I got you angry. It was good.' But I thought 'No, it wasn't.' I felt terrible!" Nevertheless, the scene is powerfully effective.

Teenage actress Katie Stuart remembers fondly her time on the show. "Everyone was very kind and made me feel very special," she recalls, "particularly Richard Dean Anderson. He kept trying to make me laugh — and usually did. Amanda and Teryl were very sweet, they really did make me feel like part of their family and, professionally, I learned so much."

COR-AI

Teal'c faces his past.

When the SG-1 team visit P3X1279, home to a race called the Bysra, one of the residents recognises Teal'c as Apophis's First Prime and accuses him of murdering his father. O'Neill and the rest of the team must persuade Teal'c's accuser, the Council of Ancients and the Jaffa himself that the death sentence is not appropriate in this case.

Written by:
Tom J. Astle
Directed by:
Mario Azzopardi

Guest cast:
Peter Williams (Apophis), David McNally (Hanno), Paulina Gillis (Byrsa Woman), Christina Jastrzembska (Member of the Council of Ancients), Michasa Armstrong (Shak'l)

O'Neill (to Daniel): "Why does it always have to be a religious thing with you? Couldn't they just be coming from a swap meet?"

"THIS WAS SUCH A cool episode to do," announces Christopher Judge. The deeper significance of the story has a strong appeal to the actor. "It really cut to the quick of Teal'c's whole ideology," Judge continues. "And that is: 'You are ultimately responsible for your actions, and you have to be ready to face the consequences, no matter what position you later find yourself in.' There's a great line where Teal'c says, 'I'm sorry O'Neill. I will not run.' And to me that is the very core of Teal'c. He believes — 'I did this. Even though I was following orders and serving Apophis when I killed Hanno's father, I am still responsible for that man's death. The victims of that attack deserve to extract whatever revenge for my bad deed that they think is due to me. If I am a man, then I have to sit there and accept it.' It's a matter of honour and honesty above everything else, which to me describes exactly what Teal'c is about. I think the audience really got to see that, probably for the first time, in 'Cor-Ai'. The message to me was that, though anyone can change, you're still held accountable for your actions and it's not enough just to say, 'Hey! I'm a different person now.'"

On a lighter note, Judge also remembers: "I got to take my shirt off! It's a common thread in all the episodes that I enjoy. I'm not sure what that means!" He further admits, "I spent the scene where the women are preparing my body giggling my ass off. I've come to the conclusion that Teal'c was a nudist on Chulak!"

Enigma

The US government place the Tollan under lockdown.

Written by:
Katharyn Powers
Directed by:
William Gereghty

Guest cast:
Tobin Bell (Omoc), Garwin Sanford (Narim), Tom McBeath (Colonel Mayborne), Gerard Plunkett (Tuplo), Gary Jones (Technician), Frida Betrani (Lya)

Rescued from certain death, the Tollan leader, Omoc, demands to be sent to a world where their advanced knowledge can be appreciated. However, Narim – a friendly Tollan – lets slip that Omoc's father once shared Tollan advancements with a civilisation like Earth, leading to a civil war that destroyed the primitive planet and destabilised the Tollan.

Carter: "Air — in pockets from 1500 down to 200 degrees."
O'Neill: "Sounds like LA."

"'ENIGMA' WAS AN INTERESTING episode because it introduced the Tollan to us," says Brad Wright. Acknowledging that they were a pretty miserable bunch, he continues, "They have become the allies who won't give us anything. This story was when we looked the Prime Directive [*Star Trek*'s famous 'non-interference' law] in the face, except we were the ones who failed to benefit from the Tollan Prime Directive! The Tollan had the Prime Directive, and we were pissed off by that. I mean, we had saved them from death by volcano!" Hinting at some appearances in later seasons, Wright confirms, "We did make a good friend in Narim. I think it's great that a character like his can come back over the course of the show, which is a significant amount of time, and renew their acquaintance with us. To the general audience he may be just a guy, but for the fans it helps them recognise that we have a bit of a 'fabric' going. A fan actually described what we're trying to do here by writing on the internet, '*Stargate SG-1* may not be the best show on television, but it is something of a rather meaty novel. It's a novel that has got hundreds and hundreds of chapters but remembers where the book began.' *Stargate* has had the continuity of myself and Robert Cooper making sure that characters like Narim come back, and that the Tollan are still the Tollan, as opposed to some other strange race, and I think all of us have benefited from that."

SOLITUDES

Comrades in arms.

O'Neill and Carter are trapped in an icy wilderness after their trip through the Stargate goes badly wrong. Seriously injured, O'Neill fights to stay alive whilst Carter struggles with the nearby Stargate. Back at Stargate Command, Teal'c and Daniel are working around the clock to try to decipher where in a million worlds their compatriots could be.

Written by:
Brad Wright
Directed by:
Martin Wood

Guest cast:
Gary Jones (Technician), Dan Shea (Sergeant Siler)

Carter: "Colonel?"
O'Neill: "It's my side arm, I swear. No giggling."

AS FAR AS SAM Carter's alter ego is concerned, the scene where she and O'Neill share body heat to keep warm was "a major coup for the writers who discovered their sense of humour: it was not an ad-lib. That 'side arm' line was actually written in there." Amanda Tapping also recalls her own heroic efforts to lighten things up: "There is a scene at the DHD when O'Neill comes crawling up, his leg broken, and director Martin Wood suggested I had some fun with the shot, because it was freezing cold and we were all miserable. So Rick says, 'Can you dig it out?' and he is expecting me to reply something like, 'If we can't, we can use the chipped ice we melt for drinking water.' But I yelled, 'Can we dig it out? You spent seven years on *MacGyver* and you can't figure this out?' Rick's eyes got really big, but I just carried on, 'God! We've got a belt buckle, a shoelace, a stick of gum... build us a nuclear reactor for crying out loud! You used to be MacGadget, MacGimmick. Now you're just MacUseless,' and then wailed away about being stuck on a glacier with MacGyver. It was hilarious...

"I got to take an amazing helicopter ride up to Pemberton Icefield," Tapping continues. "They literally plonked me on this icefield, and then the helicopter flew up further away so they could shoot a long lens whilst I crawled into a crevasse and out again. At the time I kept thinking, 'Ohmigod! I am never going to get the opportunity to do this again.'"

Tin Man

The real SG-1 – or machines?

Written by:
Jeff King
Directed by:
Jimmy Kaufman

Guest cast:
Teryl Rothery (Dr Fraiser), Jay Brazeau (Harlan)

Rendered unconscious by an electrical trap on PX3989, SG-1 awake to find that Harlan, an elderly native of the planet, has repaired their damaged bodies. On their return to the SGC, the team discovers that their human bodies have been replaced by machines. SG-1 return to the planet where Harlan introduces SG-1 to 'themselves', with hilarious but also touching results.

O'Neill: "What, this is better – I'm dead?"

"THIS WAS SUCH A fun episode to do," says Michael Greenburg. "Jay Brazeau is a brilliant actor and can really use a comic beat."

"Jon Glassner and I were flying back from LA," recalls Brad Wright, "and we had to solve a problem, because Jeff King wanted to turn the team into robots, but we didn't know how to end it. The whole notion that we were trying to solve through the episode was, 'How do we get back into our bodies?' The brainstorm I had was that SG-1 hadn't been transferred into the robots — they had been copied. I thought it was really cool that we weren't even following 'our' characters through the episode, but one hundred per cent copies of them instead."

One of the Wright's favourite scenes is when O'Neill leaves O'Neill: "Rick really enjoyed the challenge of predicting his own rhythms, and imagining what it was like to respond to himself. Don't forget he would do one side, then the camera was locked off, and he would change costume and go do the other side. There were hours and hours in between but he had to respond as if it had just happened."

"The episode has a big place in my heart because it was the first time we'd gone for out-and-out comedy," Wright adds. "Before 'Tin Man' we were allowing the humour to come through, but within a serious story. This was the first time we let a guest character be balls-out funny." Clearly a fan of the actor, Wright grins, "Jay Brazeau is a local Vancouver actor and I wrote Harlan for him."

There But For the Grace of God

Jackson accidentally activates the doorway to an alternative universe during an exploratory mission to P3R233. Earth is under attack by Goa'uld forces that are about to capture Stargate Command. Teal'c is still First Prime to Apophis and there's more than just a working relationship between Carter and O'Neill. Unable to prevent the total annihilation of the peoples of this world, Daniel must find a way to get back to his own reality to prevent the same thing happening there.

Story by:
David Kemper
Teleplay by:
Robert C. Cooper
Directed by:
David Warry-Smith

Guest cast:
Elizabeth Hoffman (Catherine Langford), Gary Jones (Technician), Stuart O'Connell (Marine), Michael Kopsa (News Anchor)

Jackson: "Unless the last two years have been a wacky, wacky dream I am a member of SG-1."

THINGS MAY HAVE SEEMED like a wacky dream to the team's archaeologist, but for Amanda Tapping this episode was more a dream come true. "I got to have hair!" she laughs. On a more serious note, the actress confides that the farewell scene between the alternative O'Neill and Carter was actually written as a kiss, but says, "We looked at each other and said, 'Let's make it a hug.'" Tapping suggests, "I actually think the hug was much better than a kiss — to me it conveyed a much deeper level of feeling." Of her co-star she says, "I am so glad we were both on the same page with it. It's not that I didn't want to kiss Richard Dean Anderson — I did want to! Just don't tell anybody."

Gary Jones beams, "My character got to fire a machine gun." Jones recounts, "One of the crew handed me a fully automatic weapon and asked if I'd fired one before. I said, 'Wow, are you kidding? No!' So we went out to the parking lot, he handed me a pair of ear defenders, put a blank clip in the gun and told me to fire away. I couldn't hear a thing, but there were sparks flying out from the side of the gun! When we were ready to shoot the scene I stood between Don Davis and three huge stunt men. The sound, when we started firing, was unbelievable. That's one of the reasons why I love coming on the show — you never know quite what you're in for when you turn up for work."

A distraught Daniel watches an Earth's demise.

Politics

Daniel tries to save the world.

Written by:
Brad Wright
Directed by:
Martin Wood

Guest cast:
Ronny Cox (Senator Kinsey), Robert Wisden (Lieutenant Colonel Samuels)

Daniel is determined that the information he obtained on the alternative Earth be used to prevent cataclysmic disaster on our planet. However, whilst the Goa'uld stalk towards this Earth reality, the SG-1 team must deal with the powerful chairman of the Appropriations Committee who wants to bury the Gate and close the programme.

O'Neill: "Engaged?"
Carter: "Theoretically it's possible."
O'Neill: "It's against regulations."

BRAD WRIGHT ADMITS THAT 'Politics' was "unashamedly a clip show, which almost always happens in the first season of a show with a pilot as big as ours — it was designed to save money. I have done several clip shows (not something I'm particularly proud of), and one of the things I've learned is to get a star — and we had a great one in Ronny Cox." As well as having a great guest star, Wright insists the only way forward is to "create a story that stands alone even if you don't see the clips."

"Before we put the clips in," Wright explains, "I edited and made a tight little episode. Granted it was only twenty-six minutes long so the remainder needed to be clips, but I knew what they were going to be. The goal was to create a good dynamic. The other rule I have is that I don't have a clip in the pre-credits 'tease', act one, or act five, so the audience doesn't know it's a clip show until they are fully on board."

Wright confirms, "Some people feel a little bit ripped off. With clip shows, fans are seeing things they've seen before, but the person who has never watched the show before — they don't mind that at all. But what I tried to do, and what I think Ronny delivered very nicely, was a really good performance leading to a cliffhanger. It was also the beginning of Ronny's participation in *Stargate SG-1*, and it's great for us to have a recurring character of his calibre."

Within the Serpent's Grasp

When the Goa'uld decide to stake a claim to Earth, the team head through the Stargate to try to prevent the attack. They find themselves on an enemy ship full of Jaffa warriors, unable to dial home. Left with no choice Carter and Jackson set as many explosives as they can around the ship. Meanwhile O'Neill and Teal'c see Skaara, now the host to Klorel, Apophis's son. Their only hope is the possibility that Skaara's strength of spirit will enable him to temporarily conquer the Goa'uld that inhabits his body.

Story by: James Crocker
Teleplay by: Jonathan Glassner
Directed by: David Warry-Smith

Guest cast: Peter Williams (Apophis), Gary Jones (Technician), Alexis Cruz (Skaara/Klorel), Brent Stait (Major Ferretti)

O'Neill: "I always get a happy, tingly feeling when I see those guys."

BOTH BRAD WRIGHT AND Jonathan Glassner are happy to confess that the fans of the show were responsible for a major change of plan. "As far as we were concerned the Skaara character was dead," begins Glassner. "We'd hinted that we were going to kill him, and we actually did... " Brad Wright continues, "But we'd started getting the message from fans that he was a really popular character and we thought, 'Boy, if we kill him, they are going to kill us!'" Glassner goes on, "In fact, when news of the character's death leaked out, the fans went ballistic. They were furious. We didn't think they would care that much, but the volume of mail convinced us Skaara had to stay. So, thanks to the visual effects guys, we digitally cut him out of a previous scene and pasted him into one that was supposedly after he would have been dead, to show that he was alive and was going to get away. Toward the end of the episode, when Apophis makes his escape, it looks as though Klorel/Skaara is standing behind him in the rings that will whisk him to safety — but he wasn't there originally! Thank God we didn't kill him off, because we went on to do a bunch of great episodes with Alexis."

A firm favourite with the fans, Richard Dean Anderson adds his approval of the episode, saying, "It was really cool. We used the Gate, we were out in space, it had bad guys, good guys and a cliffhanger. I loved it."

Teal'c and O'Neill coming up on Earth.

Season Two

Regular Cast:

Richard Dean Anderson (Colonel Jack O'Neill)

Michael Shanks (Dr Daniel Jackson)

Amanda Tapping (Captain Samantha Carter)

Christopher Judge (Teal'c)

Don S. Davis (General Hammond)

Serpent's Lair

A Death Glider escapes an exploding Goa'uld mothership.

Written by:
Brad Wright
Directed by:
Jonathan Glassner

Guest cast:
Peter Williams (Apophis), Tony Amendola (Bra'tac), Gary Jones (Technician), Alexis Cruz (Skaara/Klorel), Robert Wisden (Lieutenant Colonel Samuels)

With Earth facing total annihilation from a fleet of Goa'uld warships, it is left to those at Stargate Command to try and save the human race. SG-1 go through the gate and embark on a daring mission. Inadvertently boarding one of the incoming ships, commanded by Klorel, adopted son of Apophis, the team realise the only solution is to blow up the ship to save the planet.

O'Neill: "Call me a pessimist, but I think it's time for a new plan."

"REMEMBER THE SCENE WHERE O'Neill and Bra'tac are getting ready to blast off in the glider?" asks Tony Amendola. "Well, to shoot that they had us on a platform, about twelve feet off the ground, and because we were supposed to be blasted out into space, they had to secure the hatch above us — not just for dramatic purposes but in a practical sense too, because there was going to be turbulence, and we had a big wind machine blowing sand in our faces. So they put this glass top over us and screwed it shut, so you can imagine it got a little claustrophobic.

"Of course, they always say it's only going to be twenty minutes. Two hours and twenty minutes later we were still there, but it was great because I thought, 'Whatever I'm going through, I know that one of the producers is sitting right next to me, going through it too. It was a great bonding experience for Richard Dean Anderson and I. We sang songs and had a little chat. Richard made me feel really at home there."

Visual effects supervisor John Gajdecki reveals how the spectacular scene with the SG-1 team slipping from the Serpent's Lair was achieved: "Death Glider models were built for that final sequence as our heroes escape from the exploding Goa'uld motherships. Each model was approximately two and a half feet in wingspan, and these miniatures were shot against a green screen using motion control techniques. Subtle camera moves and reflections were added in post production to make the shots seemingly and seamlessly match the surrounding footage."

In the Line of Duty

Teal'c and Daniel must save Captain Carter.

Whilst on the planet Nasya, Carter's body is invaded by a Goa'uld symbiote. Back on Earth, only Cassandra, who has Naquadah in her blood, can sense the Goa'uld within Sam. Captured and imprisoned, the Goa'uld finally reveals its identity as Jolinar of Malkshur, a member of a rebel Goa'uld group the Tok'ra, who oppose the System Lords' practice of subduing other races. It also announces that an assassin is hunting it, and will not hesitate to kill Carter to get to Jolinar unless stopped by SG-1.

Written by:
Robert C. Cooper
Directed by:
Martin Wood

Guest cast:
Teryl Rothery (Dr Fraiser), Katie Stuart (Cassandra), Judy Norton (Talia), Peter Lacroix (Ashrak)

Teal'c: "When you speak to her, do not see your friend."

IT MAY HAVE STARTED off as a cost-cutting exercise, but 'In the Line of Duty' became one of the pivotal episodes of the series. Jonathan Glassner explains: "When we originally came up with the idea, it was going to be a 'bottle show', which means it's made just using our regular sets. But then we proceeded to shoot the 'teaser', which — much to the chagrin of the studio — was expensive, because of all the attacks and fly-pasts and extra cast members. I guess we strayed from the original purpose of saving money, but we had too much fun making the teaser to cut back on anything else!

"This episode is the first time we mention the Tok'ra. The Tok'ra came out of a need in that episode to give us a moral and ethical ambiguity on what to do about the Goa'uld that had taken over Carter. Introducing the Tok'ra basically changed the whole series."

"I found that really hard," Amanda Tapping volunteers. "I just remember stillness and being really dark. I was in a very dark place, and it was particularly difficult to do the scene where Sam first comes into the Gateroom raging because I'd never shown that type of anger with Carter. The tossing O'Neill aside part was a lot of fun, but for the most part it was very difficult. Michael, Christopher and Richard were trying to make me laugh in the darkest scene, because each of them had an individual moment with me and they tried to lighten it for me. I just remember trying to get a different physicality for her."

Prisoners

Written by:
Terry Curtis Fox
Directed by:
David Warry-Smith

Guest cast:
Bonnie Bartlett (Linea), Colin Lawrence (Major Warren), Andrew Whekler (Major Stan Kovacek), Mark Acheson (Vishnor), Michael Puttonen (Simian), Colleen Winton (Dr Greene)

After helping a man who turns out to be a fleeing murderer, the team are condemned to spend the rest of their days in a penal colony. SG-1 are surprised to find the place ruled by a frail-looking woman called Linea. Working together, SG-1 and Linea devise a plan for escape and manage to make it back to Earth. But events come full circle as the 'one good turn' motto is put to the test once more, with unexpected and frightening results.

Linea: "There are many forms of power, my dear, some more subtle than others."

"SMOKING SHOES, GRUEL OUT of a trough, big, tough, hairy guys — yeah, I remember that one," grins John Smith. "It was a really dark and grimy set but everyone had fun. Rick has a great sense of humour so there were a lot of heehaws that week." Amanda Tapping laughs, "It was all about dirt! In 'Prisoners' we had all these amazing extras — really big, freaky looking guys. It was dirty, dark and smelly, and we were surrounded by these scary looking guys. It was cool!"

It might have been a blast, but it was also a major pain for the producers of the show. "We had a problem when we built that dark, dirty set on the sound stage because it ended up taking around three or four weeks to get all of that dirt out of everything!" explains Jonathan Glassner. "The whole place was filthy. We used dry dirt, when we should have used mud, so it would stick to stuff. Because it was dust, every time anyone took a step, it would kick up clouds of it everywhere.

"'Prisoners' was an opportunity to show that our guys don't always get it right," Glassner suggests. "With one character in particular, our people screwed up and let her get away, and she will show up again in some form or other. But we didn't want to be unrealistic, and have the team find her in the next episode, because if she can hide from every species including the Goa'uld, she can outwit our guys for a time. She got away with some pretty nasty stuff, but we will find her!"

Carter contemplates SG-1's incarceration.

The Gamekeeper

Teal'c instructs the Gamekeeper in the error of his ways.

The team travel to P7J989, and find themselves trapped. They wake up to a 'virtual' reality controlled by the mysterious Keeper, who forces them to relive painful moments from their lives over and over. Told by the Keeper that the outside world has been made uninhabitable by pollution, other "residents" of the planet have been kept "under wraps" for over a thousand years. SG-1 must find a way to free the residents and themselves before past memories drive them insane...

Story by: Jonathan Glassner & Brad Wright
Teleplay by: Jonathan Glassner
Directed by: Martin Wood

Guest cast: Dwight Shultz (The Keeper), Teryl Rothery (Dr Fraiser), Jay Acovone (Kawalsky), Michael Rogers (Colonel John Michaels), Lisa Bunting (Claire Jackson), Robert Duncan (Melburn Jackson)

The Keeper: "I am the Keeper of all that is, was and will be."

JONATHAN GLASSNER IS VERY pleased with the way this episode turned out: "'The Gamekeeper' came out of an idea we had way back when we were developing the stories. We didn't think we had expanded on the characters' back stories enough, and we pondered how to do that without either going back in time, or having them sit around talking about it! Eventually we came up with a video game scenario, which gave us a way of exploring the death of Jackson's parents in sort of a sci-fi way." Michael Shanks says, "It went some way to showing why Daniel is the way he is, and it was a challenge to make it all make sense."

"There's this big Dome in Vancouver — the Observatory in Queen Elizabeth Park," Glassner continues. "It's basically a really big greenhouse surrounded by beautiful gardens, and when anyone came to visit me in Vancouver I would take them there for Saturday brunch. One time I was there I realised — we had to use it as a set! We didn't think we could get it, because it's very protected; the eco-system is very delicate and fragile. But I wrote the episode as if we were going to film there, and then actually persuaded them to go for it. It turned out that one of the people in charge was a huge fan of the show and he said, 'Sure! Just don't touch any of the plants.'" Glassner is keen to point out that all of the plants the cast do touch in the episode were put there by the production designers and crew!

Need

Daniel bids Shyla a fond farewell.

Written by:
Robert C. Cooper & Damian Kindler
Directed by:
Robert C. Cooper

Guest cast:
Teryl Rothery (Dr Fraiser), Heather Hanson (Shyla), George Touliatos (Pyrus)

On the planet P3R636, Daniel comes to the aid of a princess as she attempts to throw herself from a cliff-top. He and the team are set to work in Naquadah mines by her irate father. After sustaining serious injury, Daniel is looked after by the princess. Daniel tries to secure the freedom of the rest of SG-1, but an irresistible temptation could scupper all their plans.

Carter: "Lately I get this weird feeling when I'm near Teal'c."
O'Neill: "Who doesn't?"

"THIS WAS ANOTHER DIRTY episode," grins Amanda Tapping. "Rick already had make-up dirt on him, but then he'd go round and pick up dirt from the floor and wipe it all over himself, and anyone else nearby. We were all filthy. I remember going home, washing my hair and laughing at the colour of the water in the sink. It was great fun though. I love getting dirty more than getting pretty!"

Michael Shanks reacts with laughter to the compliment that he played the part of an addict with considerable aplomb. He insists, "I'm not going to comment on that," before going on to shrug, "it was one of those things. It was early on in the second season and is another one of those episodes where I look back and think 'Ohmigod! I was terrible in that.'

"It's tough to fully comment on that show," Shanks continues, "because I'm apt to think about how I would have played a particular scene in a different way to improve on the performance I gave, which is what I tend to do with a lot of my work. Looking back though, I think there were some nice moments. 'Need' was a good character episode."

Shanks also feels the story was one of the strongest to highlight the bond between Jack O'Neill and his team. "The scene toward the end, where O'Neill puts his life on the line to support Daniel physically and mentally," he notes, "shows how far their friendship has evolved from the days when O'Neill just thought of Daniel as a geek."

Thor's Chariot

Returning to Cimmeria, which is now under attack from the Goa'uld, SG-1 meet up with Gairwyn and her friend Olaf. On their initial visit to the planet the team destroyed Thor's Hammer, its only defence against the Goa'uld. Whilst O'Neill and Teal'c find themselves confronting the enemy head-on, Carter, Jackson and Gairwyn return to the Hall of Thor's Might where the trio find themselves facing a series of tests set by a hologram of Thor, the Asgard god who supposedly guards the planet.

Written by:
Katharyn Powers
Directed by:
William Gereghty

Guest cast:
Tamsin Kelsey (Gairwyn), Andrew Kavadas (Olaf), Douglas H. Arthurs (Heru-ur), Mark Gibbon (Thor)

Daniel Jackson: "I don't suppose this is the best time to bring up my problem with heights?"

VISUAL EFFECTS SUPERVISOR JAMES Tichenor is understandably proud of the effects in 'Thor's Chariot', saying, "I really liked the floor drop-away shot, which was done in conjunction with Rainmaker Digital Pictures. It was one of those things where we were wondering whether or not we could do it, because it was such a dynamic simulation, and is something that we would generally shoot using a model. Being a TV show with a TV budget meant that was out of the question, so we simulated it all in CG. The pit was a matte painting that was done by Kent Matheson. When Gairwyn was walking along the beam and we were looking down on her, she was actually only five inches off the ground! We had green screen on either side of her, painted all of that away and put the pit in. The angles where we're looking from the pit up to her, we put the platform up about six feet, so you get the idea that she could fall off the beam."

Recalling the trepidation he felt at the start of the episode, Tichenor smiles when he remembers the result: "When we showed it to Jonathan Glassner, who had been warned the effect was so difficult to achieve he might not get quite what he expected, he took one look at it, said, 'Great!' and moved on. That felt really good."

Solving riddles – Asgard style.

MESSAGE IN A BOTTLE

Story by:
Michael Greenburg & Jarrad Paul
Teleplay by:
Brad Wright
Directed by:
David Warry-Smith

Guest cast:
Teryl Rothery (Dr Fraiser), Tobias Mehler (Lieutenant Graham Simmons), Gary Jones (Technician), Dan Shea (Sergeant Siler), Kevin Conway (SG Leader)

The team bring an orb back through the Stargate. During tests to try and determine its self-sufficient power source, the orb seems to destabilise and they decide to return it through the Gate. However, the orb suddenly shoots bolts across the room, pinning O'Neill to the wall through his shoulder. Organisms begin to infect both O'Neill and crucial SGC computer systems, as the organisms initiate the base self-destruct countdown, Carter suggests they try to communicate with the device.

Teal'c: "Undomesticated equines could not remove me."
O'Neill: "... That's a joke. You told a joke... Don't make me laugh."

"YOU KNOW THOSE TIME capsules?" asks co-writer Michael Greenburg. "Well, my big 'what if' with this episode was, 'What if another planet built a time capsule, but instead of a box, it was an orb that actually contained everything about that planet? All the information about the peoples, the technology — even its surviving beings — were somehow put in this orb. But the reason the whole world went into the orb was because the planet was unfit to live on any more.' Kind of what would happen to Earth if we just ran it helter-skelter without any conservation or environmental awareness. So, their world was dead, and the team find the orb and bring it back — and it likes Earth and wants to stay! That was the seed of the idea and we just played off that. Rick did a fantastic job, because he was impaled on a wall for most of the episode and it was tough! But the tough ones are always worth it in the end."

Supervisor John Gajdecki and co-ordinator Simon Lacey worked on the visual effects for the episode, and colleague James Tichenor is full of praise for the results they achieved: "There's a shot where one of the legs of the device shoots through O'Neill's shoulder and pins him back to the wall. Stunt man Dan Shea was attached to an ascender rig that drove him into the wall, we then mapped Rick's face from a green screen shoot onto Dan's body — so it's really a head replacement."

O'Neill and Teal'c restrain their sense of humour.

FAMILY

Teal'c: a Jaffa warrior on Chulak.

On Teal'c's home world of Chulak SG-1 learn that his son has been kidnapped by Apophis, who was presumed dead. Teal'c's homecoming is not quite as he expected: his wife Drey'auc has re-married and when they find his son, Rya'c, he has been brainwashed by the System Lord and brands his own father a traitor. Helped by Bra'tac, the Jaffa's former mentor, the team struggle to de-programme the boy, outwit Apophis and restore familial relations.

Written by:
Katharyn Powers
Directed by:
William Gereghty

Guest cast:
Teryl Rothery (Dr Fraiser), Tony Amendola (Bra'tac), Peter Williams (Apophis), Brook Parker (Drey'auc), Neil Denis (Rya'c), Peter Bryant (Fro'tak), Jan Frandsen (Dj'nor), Laara Sadiq (Female Technician)

Fro'tak: "I am Fro'tak of the High Cliffs."
O'Neill: "Jack — of the Windy City."

CHRISTOPHER JUDGE REMEMBERS THIS episode because it gave him another chance to work with Tony Amendola as Bra'tac, Teal'c's Jaffa mentor. "Tony is just 'The Man'," says Judge. "He has a real presence. It's a pleasure to share a scene with him." Judge is also pleased with how the tensions between Teal'c and his family were handled: "I loved the way you got to see Teal'c display some strong emotion. You saw him being jealous and what lengths he would go to, to save his family." Discussing the scene in which Teal'c tried to attack his former best friend for running off with his wife, Judge is asked if he really got into the part, and stalked around being rotten to the poor actor who had to cross him, Judge grins, "Naw! There were no such shenanigans on that one. It was a big episode for me. I'm only a disruptive force when it's someone else's episode!

"At first, Teal'c was totally focused on freeing his people," Judge notes. "But in 'Family' he puts his wife and son first. Teal'c refuses to believe that his son could fall under Apophis's influence. Teal'c's persistence finally pays off when Rya'c fights the brain-washing."

As irrepressible as ever, Mr Judge winks, "When you see Teal'c turn and smile as he takes his family back through the gate, it's because he knows he's going off for some 'marital relations' — if you know what I'm saying..."

Dr Daniel Jackson

Daniel Jackson: "Colonel O'Neill thinks I'm a geek. I have no idea how to get us back. I'll never get paid."

The task of re-inventing a character well known and loved from another medium has always been a bit of an uphill struggle, but it's one actor Michael Shanks approached with relish. Invited to re-create the role of Dr Daniel Jackson, the dedicated linguist and scientist left behind on the remote planet of Abydos at the end of the *Stargate* feature film, Shanks was delighted to be given the opportunity to make the character his own. Shanks is the first to admit that though initially briefed to stick closely to the original characterisation, over the course of the series he's consciously made the break from actor James Spader's original interpretation of the archaeologist in the movie, and has developed him very much in his own mould. It took a while, though. "I initially decided to stick with James Spader's portrayal first and foremost because it worked well," he explains. "The other consideration was the perception that viewers don't like too many changes all at once when it comes to favourite characters. So I went along with the wisdom at the time, which was to stick close to how the original character was played."

Shanks describes his character as "a dreamer. An ideologist who has a love of humanity and life in general. He's an eternal optimist, the kind of guy who is always looking for the best in people and situations. Daniel is always looking for answers," he continues. "He needs to know who we are, how we got here and why." This continual thirst for knowledge has led him into some dangerous places. In 'The Torment of Tantalus', Daniel is ready to risk everything, including his life, to find out more about the "meaning of life stuff."

Shanks' decision to pursue a career in acting wasn't a spur of the moment whim: "I started off doing Commercial Studies at university and then realised that all I really wanted to do was perform." Changing courses, he graduated with a Bachelor of Fine Arts degree from the University of British Columbia before being whisked off to the other side of Canada to work at the Stratford Shakespeare Festival in Ontario. Guest spots on television and in films soon followed. He made his film début in *Call of the Wild* and featured in series such as *The Commish*, *Highlander* and *The Outer Limits* before taking up his appointment with Dr

Daniel Jackson. "I have a very short attention span," he grins, "so keep my hand in with other projects when not filming *Stargate SG-1*. I love the 'rush' you get when you perform on stage, so I played Hamlet for five weeks, and I've done a couple of independent movies."

An intensely private man off the set, the fact that the locals in Vancouver are used to the city being an extended film set, and see actors wandering around all the time, suits Shanks down to the ground. "People here are pretty blasé about all this star stuff, and don't really bother you. Fortunately, once I take off Daniel's glasses and hat I have the kind of looks that blend in with everybody else. I only tend to get recognised if I'm with the others, especially Christopher Judge. He walks around with Teal'c's tattoo on his forehead!" he jokes. His friend Judge laughs, "Shanks will soon have reached celebrity recluse status." The actor does sneak the odd look at fan websites, though he doesn't get involved in 'chats', offering, "It's not that I don't want to, I just prefer to hold on to a little bit of mystery."

O'Neill to Carter: "Major, next time Daniel gets the urge to help someone, shoot him."

Asked which personality traits he feels he shares with the character he plays, Shanks says, "There's a lot of me in Daniel. Daniel has a lot more curiosity, but I guess I would describe myself as stubborn, enthusiastic, genuine, naive and playful." Shanks feels the relationships between his character and the other members of SG–1 have deepened over the course of the series, allowing Daniel to become more of a team player. "I think there will always be that slight antagonism between Daniel and Jack, because of the very nature of their personalities," he says, adding, "his bond with Teal'c and Sam Carter is being allowed to develop, although I'd like to see more of that."

The friendships between the cast members have been close from day one. A quiet but deadly joker on set, Shanks' impressions of characters from *The Simpsons* have caused his co-stars to 'corpse' on many occasions. Christopher Judge reveals that he is still thinking of ways to pay back the many practical jokes Shanks has played on him. "I'm too scared to tell you what they are," whispers Judge. "You don't know what he'll do to retaliate in the future!"

Discussing how the character has evolved through the series, Shanks says, "Although Daniel is still very passionate about what he does and how he goes about things, he's grown up a lot. When Sha're was first taken, his all-consuming desire was to find her and get her back. In season three, the events in 'Forever in a Day' take that possibility away, and whilst it's a tragedy of sorts, the introduction of the Harsesis child gives Daniel a whole new purpose."

Charged with finding and protecting Sha're's son, Shanks suggests this mission gives him the chance to explore the bittersweet nature of the task. "Daniel has to face up to the challenge of keeping a promise to someone he loved very much, whilst having to swallow the fact that the child was sired by the one person he hates most in the universe. Fortunately, 'Maternal Instinct' gave Daniel the opportunity to let go of that hate and keep his promise. It was quite a turning point for him."

Like Jack O'Neill, Michael Shanks is quite the cynic and the similarity between Shanks and O'Neill naturally seeps into the relationship between Shanks and Richard Dean Anderson. "I love the banter that's developed between my character and Rick's," Shanks beams. "Towards the middle of season one we discovered that we had the same irreverent sense of humour, and the writers began writing little snippets to let us play with that. Some of the fans have felt that this intimated some sort of rift between us, but it's not like that at all. It's an opportunity for us to have fun, and show there's a deeper understanding between us than is totally evident on the surface."

Empathy aside, O'Neill did try to bump Daniel off in 'Absolute Power'. "Oh yeah! But that was a hoot to do," laughs Shanks. "When the producers came to me and asked how I felt about Daniel being perceived as the bad guy for a change I jumped at the chance. It was a wonderful opportunity to show how the Daniel we see every week could behave given a different set of circumstances." As for thwarting O'Neill's attempt to put an end to his shenanigans in that episode, Shanks laughs, "Rick got his own back when I was directing 'Double Jeopardy'. All the other actors were completely up for anything. They knew I was an actor's director and they understood that's what I cared about the most, but Rick is the kind of actor who doesn't take direction — period. I think he only did with me, a bit, to humour me. But I have to say that, basically, he was a pain in the micdah!"

Still smiling, Shanks concedes, "Actually, it was quite an eye-opener for me, because I'm usually the one who's

trying not to do what the director tells me to do. It was pretty funny having the boot on the other foot."

As well as progressing on the director front, seasons three and four also saw Shanks explore his bent toward writing. "Lots of people give me articles and books and the like because they think that, because I play the character, I personally am interested in archaeology. I occasionally get inundated and can't read them all, but one of our crewmembers gave me a book full of mysteries of South America. I became fascinated with the myth of the crystal skulls. One of the wonderful things about *Stargate* is if we see things like that, we can point to the stars to explain things that happened in the past, so I started to write a story about the skulls."

Shanks admits that the resulting episode 'Crystal Skull' wasn't quite as they'd expected. Nevertheless, he is delighted to have been able to follow that particular path. "From an actor's point of view, that episode had the first and only all-green screen set we've ever done, and was a very interesting process. It was funny because you couldn't move a lot. It was too expensive to have us move because it was incredibly difficult visual effects-wise to shift the background away from us to get the right depth and perspective, so we spent a lot of the time locked down. Not an easy thing to do given our natures and personalities!"

Revealing the inquisitive side of his nature, Shanks enthuses, "I'm always fascinated when we get to the end of an episode like 'Crystal Skull' and unleash mysteries that we still can't fathom. It's like *Raiders of the Lost Ark* — just when you think you've solved something, a greater mystery emerges that is beyond our comprehension. I think it's always intriguing when the answer to one thing raises questions which make you continue to explore."

Daniel: "Maybe I did some good now and again, but nothing I've ever done seems to have changed anything."

For six years archaeologist, anthropologist, best friend and workmate Daniel Jackson has been the voice of reason at the SGC. He's coaxed, persuaded and cajoled his SG-1 team mates, his boss, General Hammond, the government, the Goa'uld and indeed anyone who would listen, that much more can be achieved by studying other cultures to learn about them, rather than simply blasting a way into any given situation. His message hasn't been lost on the show's audience either. Masses of letters and e-mails arrive at the Bridge Studios every day, thanking the actor for the positive influence he's had on their lives. "It's interesting," says Shanks, "because I'm only now beginning to learn what impact the character has on the world outside the studio. He's a character that is based around the best and most idealistic of intentions. Certainly, there are things about Daniel that are strong qualities that we, as 'good' individuals, cherish. That's why I like the character so much! When I hear that Daniel's attitude toward life and the many challenges it offers has had an impact on somebody else's 'real' life — that's totally overwhelming. It's humbling. I'm not sure it's deserved but, I always say, 'If you can help someone, then do it.'"

Even though he was used to a certain amount of mail appearing on a daily basis, Shanks was completely nonplussed by the sheer volume of correspondence that deluged the studio, the programme makers and executives when he decided to leave the show. The actor was amazed at the amount of personal messages of support he received. "It was very flattering and a great barometer to indicate the character's influence in the series," he says. "That level of support certainly re-affirmed, in my mind, how valued Daniel really was. I had been feeling somewhat undervalued at that time. I felt that certain expectations hadn't been met and certain personal goals had not been achieved, so it was very flattering to receive these acknowledgments. I can't say this was my sole reason for wanting to return to the show on a regular basis for season seven, but it certainly helped focus my mind on where I wanted to be, and what I wanted to do."

SECRETS

Written by:
Terry Curtis Fox
Directed by:
Duane Clark

Guest cast:
Peter Williams (Apophis), Carmen Argenziano (General Jacob Carter), Erick Avali (Kasuf), Vaitiare Bandera (Sha're), Douglas H. Arthurs (Heru-ur), Chris Owens (Armin Selig), Michael Tiernan (Ryn'tak)

A reporter tells O'Neill that he knows what goes on inside the mountain complex, and intends to tell the world. Meanwhile, Daniel travels back to Abydos with Teal'c to explain that he has failed to find Sha're, but is amazed to find her alive, and living at home – and about to give birth to Apophis's child. Back on Earth, Sam struggles with the devastating news that her father is suffering from cancer. Daniel and Teal'c conspire to use Apophis's rivalry with another System Lord, Heru-ur, to help them escape.

O'Neill: "It's O'Neill with two 'l's. There is another Colonel O'Neil who spells his name with one 'l'. He has no sense of humour."

MANY FRIENDSHIPS DEEPENED AND new bonds were formed while filming this episode. "It was wonderful to meet Carmen Argenziano," beams Amanda Tapping. "We met at six in the morning, and by seven he was telling me his character had cancer. It was a heavily emotional scene and we had to connect, but it ended up much deeper than that. I ended up loving him. Right before the scene, I squeezed his hand and said, 'Right! Here we go.' And it went from there. Our relationship as characters grew into a genuine love between a father and daughter, much the same as it's done on a personal level. We spend time together whenever we can. I'm proud to say he and his family have welcomed me as their own and he's become part of my family."

"I liked the way the story built on the relationship between Teal'c and Daniel," says Chris Judge, "showing the depth of a friendship where Teal'c would go to great lengths, including putting some of his own feelings on hold, to support his friend. There is also an intensity between Daniel and his wife Sha're, which was really beautiful. The thing that touched me most was the way it showed Daniel, an outcast somewhat like Teal'c, finding his true love only to lose her through no fault of his own. His determination to stay true to her and to fight to get her back is a powerful lesson. I really admire Shanks for his performance in that one."

A Horus Guard searches for Apophis's child.

A big, ugly bug from planet BP63Q1.

On a mission to BP63Q1, Teal'c is stung by a giant insect. Back on Earth, the Jaffa undergoes a physical mutation brought on by the insect venom. The military brass take him from the SGC for experimentation. Teal'c escapes from the transport and goes on the run. Whilst the rest of SG-1 risk a return visit to the insect world to find a cure, it's left to a plucky young homeless girl who has befriended Teal'c to save the day.

Written by: Robert C. Cooper
Directed by: David Warry-Smith

Guest cast: Teryl Rothery (Dr Fraiser), Tom McBeath (Colonel Maybourne), Colleen Rennison (Ally)

O'Neill: "Those are bugs, sir. Big, ugly bugs."

DAVID WARRY-SMITH MAINLY REMEMBERS one thing about 'Bane': the bug. "It was a huge problem actually," he confides, "because we couldn't get the thing to stick on his shoulder. Then every time it tried flapping its wings things went a bit awry..." Chuckling, he goes on, "We CG'd it flying around the Gateroom with Rick blowing the hell out of everything. It was one of the first CG animals we used. We made the model first, then matched it with CG. It turned out very well."

"We loved doing Christopher's make-up, and creating the cocoon," recalls make-up supervisor Jan Newman. "Wray Douglas, special effects supervisor, came up with the idea of webbing and it was fabulous."

Not that Christopher Judge shares her enthusiasm. "That make-up was not a whole lot of fun," he recalls. "I hated having to sit still for hours having all those little bumps and boils put on. Jan just wanted to torture me! And the director, he kept me lying around on that hard, cold floor. I really had to suffer for my art."

Judge wasn't the only one who found filming somewhat uncomfortable. "There's a scene right at the end where my character soaks Jackson with a water gun," Judge remembers. "I couldn't resist, and Shanks had no idea what was coming. I pumped the thing up to the highest pressure and just let him have it. He was drenched, and it hurt too. The look on his face was really priceless! We used that first take in the final edit because it was just so perfect."

The Tok'ra
Part I

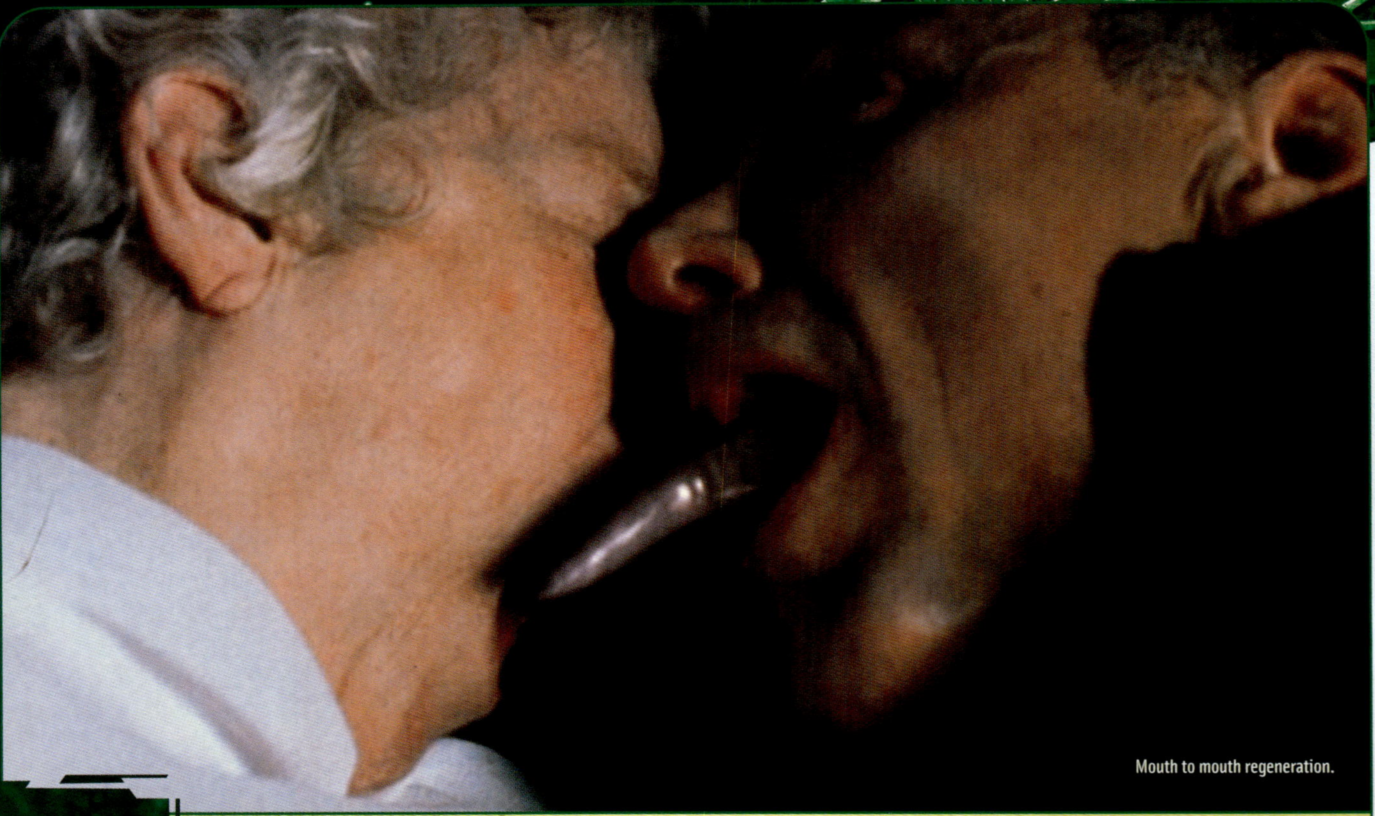

Mouth to mouth regeneration.

Written by:
Jonathan Glassner
Directed by:
Brad Turner

Guest cast:
JR Bourne (Martouf), Carmen Argenziano (Jacob Carter), Sarah Douglas (Garshaw of Belote), Winston Rekert (Cordesh), Joy Coghill (Selmak), Steve Makaj (Colonel Makepeace), Laara Sadiq (Technician Davis)

Sam Carter experiences a vivid dream where she remembers events from the life of Jolinar, the Tok'ra who inhabited her body before being killed by a Goa'uld assassin. When SG-1 travel to P34353J, they decline the Tok'ra's invite to volunteer as a host to one of their tribe, and the Tok'ra imprison them. In the spirit of reconciliation, Carter and Martouf agree to spend time together.

O'Neill to Martouf: "OK, son. But you'd better have her back by 11 o'clock."

EXPLAINING THE IDEAS BEHIND the Tok'ra, Jonathan Glassner begins, "They were an important invention. We felt that the Goa'uld were becoming very one-dimensional. They were just bad, bad, bad. I kept thinking that there had to be rebels other than the odd Jaffa that didn't agree with what the Goa'uld were doing. But that raised all kinds of interesting questions, because they were still stealing people in order to live, so how good could they be? That's what started off the idea of willing hosts. We developed the three episode arc with Carter's dad dying of cancer, which made him the perfect choice for somebody to be Tok'ra-ed."

A mutual admiration society built up between Amanda Tapping and JR Bourne whilst filming 'The Tok'ra'. "It was incredible," recalls Bourne. "From the moment we met, it was as if I'd known this woman all my life. There's a scene where we talk about Jolinar, and it's the first time I've ever been in an 'acting' situation where I wasn't acting. It just seemed so natural walking along and chatting to her, that we were both surprised when the director yelled 'cut'." Tapping concurs: "We had virtually no time to learn this seven-page scene together, but he was so lovely it just seemed to flow. When we did the whole walking sequence through the desert I remember we were having a really great conversation, there was just this instant connection. It was the same as when I met Carmen on 'Secrets' and Tamsin Kelsey in 'Thor's Hammer'. We met at six am, and were telling each other our deepest, darkest secrets by lunchtime!"

THE TOK'RA
PART II

Garshaw of Belote stands her ground.

Carter comes up with a possible solution to help Earth and the Tok'ra. Her father is dying of cancer, but if he were to act as the new host, both lives could be saved. By the time she brings her sick father to the Tok'ra world the Goa'uld have located the rebels and launched a full scale attack. The union of Jacob Carter with Selmak gets underway as the battle rages around them.

Written by:
Jonathan Glassner
Directed by:
Brad Turner

Guest cast:
JR Bourne (Martouf), Carmen Argenziano (Jacob Carter), Sarah Douglas (Garshaw of Belote), Winston Rekert (Cordesh), Joy Coghill (Selmak), Steve Makaj (Colonel Makepeace), Laara Sadiq (Technician Davis)

O'Neill: "Well General, if these were your everyday, run-of-the-mill, greasy-assed Goa'uld, they would've made us their hosts already."

JONATHAN GLASSNER HAS NOTHING but praise for the set designer and construction crew. "That big round crystal set was an amazing invention," he notes. "The problem was that we soon needed it again and because of the way the set was made, they couldn't store it. They'd trashed it, and had to reproduce it from scratch! However, the second time, they constructed it so it could be used over and over again. Which was a good thing, as we knew we'd be going back to the Tok'ra."

As writer, Glassner is personally proud of the scene when Jacob Carter receives the Goa'uld for the first time. Fans and critics alike commented that it was an extremely brave move to show two older people kissing on screen. "Well, she had to be a dying old lady," laughs Glassner, "and you don't see too many cute, young versions of those." Glassner also reveals why the Jacob character returned later in the series. "We didn't intend bringing Jacob back after this episode, but having worked with Carmen we thought he was excellent, and just had to write more for him."

The writers tried to do the same for British actress Sarah Douglas, but sadly other commitments prevented her return in the second season. "Sarah was a fantastic baddie in *V* and *Superman II*, and we wanted to play it so that it could look as though she were a bad guy — playing on the mistrust thing. She's very strong, yet very feminine. I love the look on Jack O'Neill's face when she kisses him."

Spirits

A spirit reveals its true appearance.

Written by:
Tor Alexander Valenza
Directed by:
Martin Wood

Guest cast:
Rodney A. Grant (Tonane), Roger Cross (Captain Conner), Alex Zahara (Xe'ls), Christina Cox (T'akaya), Kevin McNulty (Dr Warner), Laara Sadiq (Technician Davis)

As SG-1 prepare to go in search of the missing SG-11, a Trinium-tipped arrow flies out of the open Gate, injuring O'Neill. SG-1 discover that the missing unit have been abducted by the animal Spirits who are the guardians of the Salish Indians. When SG-11 suddenly reappear, both teams return home. However, the members of SG-11 are not all they seem...

O'Neill: "Brace yourselves, SG-11 is bopping around waving their arms together making our people disappear."

"IN ALL HONESTY, 'SPIRITS' was one of those that had some great ideas, and some really interesting moral arguments, and which read far better on paper than it ended up playing out. Which is probably why you don't hear an awful lot about it," observes Michael Shanks. "It was part of our experimental phase as we investigated how we as SG-1, and also the audience, would react to offshoots of different cultures. And I don't think that story was a particularly sensitive approach to the subject matter." Shanks candidly remarks, "I just don't think we pulled it off terribly well. We had other things on our mind, because it came around the time when Richard Dean Anderson's child was due to be born. The part where we go to the planet without O'Neill was done for a specific reason. Rick's partner Apryl was due to go into the hospital, and we panicked and changed lines to allow him to go with her. So as a result, the usual team dynamic just wasn't there. It wasn't the worst episode in the world, but I think we'd all like to draw a veil over that one."

As well as humans the production had to substitute a few animals during the shooting of 'Spirits'. Jonathan Glassner comments, "We were going to use a bear instead of a wolf, but in British Columbia it's illegal to work with trained animals that are originally from the wild. As we couldn't get a real bear or wolf, we actually went with a mixed breed of half wolf and half German Shepherd."

Touchstone

A device capable of controlling an entire world's climate is stolen from a paradise-like planet by a team posing as SG-1. As the weather on Madrona starts to deteriorate, it is up to the real SG-1 to locate the missing Touchstone. Their investigations reveal that Earth's second Stargate has been reactivated and is being used by a 'black ops' group. SG-1 race to find out just how high this deception goes in US Military command, while trying to recover the Touchstone before the inhabitants of Madrona perish.

Written by:
Sam Egan
Directed by:
Brad Turner

Guest cast:
Tom McBeath (Colonel Maybourne), Matthew Walker (Roham), Jerry Wasserman (Whitlow), Tiffany Knight (La Moor), Eric Breker (Major Reynolds)

O'Neill: "We came in peace. We expect to go in one piece."

IT WAS A VERY special week for Michael Shanks, he recalls, "The thing that stands out the most from that episode for me personally, is that it's the one we were filming when my child was born," he says. "It was 10 August 1998. To me the episode was a blur, because I was practising breathing technique, then going through all that new father angst!" Smiling at the memory he teases, "The blowing snow scene was one thing I do remember. That was interesting, but I have to admit that, though I didn't exactly ignore what was going on around me at work, I was pretty distracted. My mind was somewhere else at that point..."

The references in the episode to Area 51, the real-life, ultra-top-secret Air Force base in the Nevada desert, caused some problems with the powers-that-be, who proved rather sensitive. "Originally, in the script, we had O'Neill saying something like, 'Is this where we keep the little green men?'" Jonathan Glassner reveals. "But the Air Force has full approval of all our scripts, and they called and said, 'There are no aliens in Area 51. You can't keep that line in.' I explained that it was a joke, but they just repeated, 'There are no aliens in Area 51.' So I then asked if I could use their response in the script! We actually ended up going with O'Neill saying, 'Is this where they keep the aliens?' and the officer replies, 'There are no aliens in Area 51.' Then O'Neill looks at Teal'c and says, 'Present company excluded.'"

The King of Madrona holds the Touchstone.

Major Sam Carter

Sam Carter: "Colonel, I logged over 100 hours in enemy air space during the Gulf War. Is that tough enough for you? Or are we going to have to arm wrestle?"

The mischievous Amanda Tapping is worlds away from the rather sober Air Force ma'am seen in *Stargate SG-1*. Any of her colleagues will confirm the fact. "She's a comedienne in another life," explains Christopher Judge. "She knows exactly what to do or say — or even what not to do, to get me to laugh." Tapping protests that Judge has things the wrong way round, and that it's Judge and his cohorts that start her off. "It's usually at the end of the day," she says, "and it's usually my 'close-up', and the guys will all stand behind the camera trying to get me to crack up — which happens a lot."

Starting off as a captain then progressing to major, Carter is the lynch-pin of SG-1, the bridge between the military mind of Colonel O'Neill and the altruistic dreamer Dr Jackson. She's had to overcome many obstacles to prove her worth in the military. Carter's immediate response to her superior's jibe — "Just because my reproductive organs are on the inside doesn't mean I can't handle whatever you can" — comes as a result of having to handle many such prejudices in her chosen career. But her strength, determination and sheer professionalism have won through, and brought her to the fore. "Sam is very strong, very smart and committed to the Stargate programme almost to the point of obsession," Tapping explains. "For instance, Sam and Daniel can often be found working through the night to prove some theory or other."

Tapping feels the character has come a long way since her inception. "In the pilot, the writers had created this hard-assed feminist with a very didactic message, which I was really opposed to. But," she shrugs, "I really wanted to work on the show, so once I knew they were going to continue with the character, I approached the writers, who agreed we couldn't carry on with the gender argument. It was too boring."

By going with her own unique responses, Tapping feels she has managed to round Carter into a more fully developed personality. "I've tried to give Sam the toughness of a soldier without losing any of her femininity," the actress says, "although she's so dedicated to her job that it seems as though she has no life outside Stargate Command."

Whilst *Stargate SG-1* is the vehicle which has propelled Tapping to international recognition, she's not a newcomer to stage or screen. Since graduating from the University of Windsor School of Dramatic Art, she has appeared in numerous theatre productions including *Steel Magnolias* and *Noises Off*. A host of small screen credits include *The X-Files*, *Due South*, *Forever Night* and *The Outer Limits*.

At work or play, Tapping's warm nature and consummate professionalism are legendary. "All our cast are great," Jonathan Glassner smiles, "because we never once had to say we wouldn't write something because so-and-so wouldn't be able to play it, but that's especially the case with Amanda. She'd be given these long speeches, with all this technical jargon and 'protoplasmic blah', and it would come tripping off her tongue as though she had complete knowledge of what it meant!" In fact, Tapping does understand a lot of it. Swearing she's not a 'techno-geek' she concedes, "I like to know what I'm talking about, so I do research the technical and scientific stuff. I've learned a lot."

"You know with Amanda that she's going to be the first on set," producer John Smith testifies. "She's going to be five minutes early with a big smile on her face, every day. Not only that, but she'll be fully prepared, and have her dialogue in place."

O'Neill: "I have great confidence in you, Carter. Go back to the SGC and confuse Hammond."

Determined not to let the character become too tedious, Tapping says, "One of the things I've tried to do throughout the series is look for the interesting moments in scenes and play with them. Even something as simple as a slight facial movement can convey a part of the story. I owe it to myself as much as to the audience to flex my 'acting muscles' as much as possible, so that I'm constantly communicating little bits of Sam into the mix."

Director Martin Wood thinks Tapping is a master at the art. "Amanda is a director's delight," he smiles. "Without a doubt she is absolutely the easiest of the entire cast to work with, because she will always do whatever you ask. If you ask her to do something she will always find her own reason for it. She is also the easiest to cut to, because she's always got expression on her face. Even if the main focus is on another actor, Amanda is always acting and all the directors love her for that. She's so dependable."

Whilst Tapping agrees 'dependable' is good, one of the things she enjoys most about working on *SG-1* is that nothing is ever quite that predictable. At a time when so many of the sci-fi shows on television dance around the prospect of a romance between the main male and female characters, *Stargate* has gone against the grain and knocked the idea of a sexual liaison between Carter and O'Neill firmly on the head.

Speaking of the resolution of the 'do they/don't they love each other' debate, Tapping emphatically supports the writers' decision to 'clear the air'. "Sam and Jack were never meant to be together. Not just from a military point of view, but for all sorts of reasons. He would drive her crazy for starters! I love the way the writers brought the situation to the fore in 'Divide and Conquer' and had the courage to let them admit their love for each other, acknowledge that it was never to be and then let them get on with the rest of their lives."

The actress is proud to portray a strong female character that doesn't exactly shun male attention, and is perfectly comfortable being a single, well adjusted woman, happy with who she is and where she is in life. "A lot of the single women characters on TV today are frantically searching for Mr Right, and feel their lives are unfulfilled without him. Not Sam! Not that I want her to come across as smug or anything like that, but she can stand back and say, 'You know what? I love and am loved by my family and friends. I'm good at what I do. I like my job and the people I work with. I'm a success.'

"That to me is one of the greatest things about how Sam has developed over the years. She's grown from being the hard-assed, stereotypical 'feminist in the military' type into this strong, positive, happy female. I've had so many fans come up to me to let me know how much Sam's attitude has influenced their personal lives in a good way. It's extremely humbling to know that something I do on a television show can have that profound an effect. It makes me so proud to be a part of this show."

O'Neill to Carter: "You do have a penchant for pulling brilliant ideas out of your butt... head... when we need them."

The actress takes her job very seriously, but she's also a firm believer in the power of humour, and so undertakes these tasks in the most light-hearted way possible. Though quite often she doesn't really have much choice in the matter, particularly when it comes to the all-action gung-ho stuff, as Tapping has a lot less control over her limbs and laughter than her *Stargate* alter-ego. Known for her ability to trip over thin air, Tapping gives us a glimpse of her inability to get head, hands, feet and body working at the same time. Punctuation has been added but, as anyone who has ever had the good fortune to meet this woman will know, there was a lot of gesticulation involved and she hardly drew a breath...

DIARY OF A WOULD-BE STUNT WOMAN

By AMANDA TAPPING

Yeah! 'Smoke and Mirrors'! O'Neill is charged with murder and Sam goes off to the NID. I got to wear more normal clothes, sort of *Men In Black* stuff, and a nice pretty skirt. See – it's all about the wardrobe with me! But – what's really important about this episode is that I actually, for the first time ever in the history of six years of *Stargate*, got a stunt operator. I probably should have gotten some in the past because of the outrageous things I've done. But with this one I went up to our assistant director and said, "I'm charging down concrete steps, leaping over a wall and a building is exploding behind me. I'm pretty sure that's a stunt." So we (that's Peter Flemming, who played Barrett, and I) practised. We run to the end of this wall and we have to do a leap. Now, there is a mat in one position, and there are cameras positioned all around it and there's this whole 'Don't hit the camera, leap over here, land on this big fluffy mat' vibe. But every time we rehearsed it, as soon as I got close to the wall, I'd do this little gymnast-style hop, skip and leap. And people were like, "Amanda – just run and leap. Run, and leap. What's with the gymnast thing?" So I keep landing on the mat and I'd spring up and go, "Whoo Hoo! Six point four from the Russian judge!" which I thought was quite funny, but the crew were getting nervous: "She's gotta get this right. She has to get it." I mean, God bless the crew. I think they really like me, but they also know that I'm completely uncoordinated and therefore a great source of entertainment on a daily basis.

Anyway, I'm scared. I have to run down these concrete steps and they weren't built to code if you know what I mean, they're too narrow, but I can't back out because it's this huge shot and the whole neighbourhood has turned out. The spectators are all going, "Wow! They're going to blow up this house!" and though we won't actually blow it up, there is going to be a big explosion, which has taken all day to set up.

So – it's the last stunt of the day. The crew is trying to reassure me: "No worries, Amanda!" One of the stunt guys has grabbed hold of the end of the mat, to hold it up so that when I land I don't come sliding off the end. However on the last rehearsal I come flying at him, I land... and he literally punches me in the face because he's holding the mat and I collide with his fist. Then I'm holding my nose going "Oh crap" and he's all apologetic, saying "I was trying to help you" and I'm like "No! No! I'm an accident waiting to happen!" I then remember I have a gun in my hand, and that's something else I have to contend with.

Finally, we're all set to shoot. Go! I'm running down the stairs, everyone is watching. There's five cameras rolling – it's just the huge-est thing. I do the leap. I'm all good. I realise the camera is in front of me so I have to tuck in. I do it, land... and as I land... I smash myself in the face with my gun! I'm lying there stunned and I can feel the heat of the explosion and I'm like "Oh Boy!" I touch my face, which is all wet, and I thought it was blood. Turned out it wasn't – it was just snot. But my eyes are watering because I smashed myself on the nose.

Everyone is going, "Wow. That was fantastic!" I turned to Jack from craft service and said, "You know, just once I would like to do a stunt where I didn't incur some sort of injury." Then Dan Shea, our stunt co-ordinator and big wrench carrier comes up and says, "I've never worked with an actress who does her own stunts." I say, "Ya think I should stop?" and he replies, "Yeah. Amanda, God is sending you messages." You know what? I think next time, I'll listen.

A Matter of Time

O'Neill and Cromwell prepare to save the day.

Story by: Misha Rashovich
Teleplay by: Brad Wright
Directed by: Jimmy Kaufman

Guest cast: Marshall Teague (Colonel Cromwell), Teryl Rothery (Dr Fraiser), Tobias Mehler (Lieutenant Graham Simmons), Dan Shea (Sergeant Siler)

Whilst on a trip to P3X451, SG-10 encounters a black hole which quickly engulfs the planet. By activating the Stargate on Earth the door is literally left open for the black hole's gravitational pull to exert its deadly influence on the SGC. One member of SG-1 in particular must put aside past differences in order to help Sam Carter deflect the looming catastrophe.

Cromwell: "Is that proper military terminology? What is 'funky'?"

OCCASIONALLY PEOPLE WILL SAY that their world has been turned upside down, but it was more a case of the world being turned on its side in 'A Matter of Time'. "We literally had to build a replica of the Gateroom turned on its side," laughs John Smith, "so that we could have the two guys dangling from a rope. The ropes were meant to be hanging loose but in fact we had them stretched out tight and then we turned the camera sideways so that it looked right side up."

It certainly wasn't a picnic for the guys in question, who had to hang on for the best part of a day. "That really is Ricky and me up there on the ropes," recalls guest actor Marshall Teague. "We were about twenty or thirty feet off the ground, and Rick did all his own work — the inversion, the fall, the whole works." Explaining that he had the benefit of mountain climbing training, Teague grins, "So, I've been climbing for a lot of my life. As for ol' MacGyver — well, that guy can do anything!" On a serious note, Teague praises the ability of his fellow actor: "Rick is very agile and very athletic, although neither of us was particularly thrilled about being in a harness all day."

Although *Stargate SG-1* is noted for often having a less than serious approach to science fiction, Brad Wright feels that "every now and then we do use a straight-ahead science fiction 'high concept'. 'A Matter of Time' was one of those stories where we used a sci-fi staple — in this case a black hole — and built the episode around it."

The Fifth Race

When O'Neill peers into an alien viewing device, his brain is instantly filled with a vast amount of data. However his brain is unable to cope and O'Neill must travel through the Stargate alone in an effort to save himself. Having built a device which provides a huge surge of power to the Stargate, O'Neill sets the co-ordinates to an address which is off the starcharts. The Colonel's solo trip leads to an encounter which gives hope to more than one race in the galaxy...

Written by:
Robert C. Cooper
Directed by:
David Warry-Smith

Guest cast:
Teryl Rothery (Dr Fraiser), Tobias Mehler (Lieutenant Graham Simmons), Dan Shea (Sergeant Siler)

O'Neill: "I've lost the falatus to speak properly."

VISUAL EFFECTS SUPERVISOR JAMES Tichenor's favourite shot in 'The Fifth Race' is "the big effect right at the beginning, when O'Neill gets his head stuck in the little contraption. That was an effect where we morphed between the 'open' position, with O'Neill getting stuck, and the 'closed' position, where the whole thing wrapped around his head. It was a classic 2D CG morph, where it looked like the device came out and wrapped around him. If you look closely enough," Tichenor continues, revealing a few trade secrets, "you can actually see the point where we had to morph Rick's head as well, because when you have two different elements like that, sometimes it's difficult to make it look like the actor is actually interacting with the CG element in the shot. When the device was in its 'open' position, and hadn't wrapped round Rick's head all the way, he would have had to stay utterly stock still during filming to allow us to achieve the effect properly — it was easier to make his head CG as well! Then, when it was in the 'closed' position, we can't see Rick at all because the thing is covering his face. We had to spend a lot of time considering how we were going to cover both sides, and what was the most cost efficient way of doing it. It seems like a pretty simple shot, but it took a lot of effort to get it looking that interesting. It almost has the feeling of a hand coming out of the wall. It's cool!"

O'Neill, about to become the fount of all knowledge.

Serpent's Song

Written by:
Katharyn Powers
Directed by:
Peter DeLuise

Guest cast:
Teryl Rothery (Dr Fraiser), Peter Williams (Apophis), JR Bourne (Martouf), Tobias Mehler (Lieutenant Graham Simmons), Peter Lacroix (Ashrak)

SG-1 travel to a desert world, where they witness a damaged spaceship plunge to the ground in a ball of flame. Amongst the wreckage they discover a battered and bleeding Apophis. Back on Earth, in return for a new host, the Snake tempts them with the offer of all his knowledge. O'Neill refuses, whereupon the duplicitous Apophis reveals that he is being hunted down by his arch enemy Sokar. Martouf of the Tok'ra advises his friends to return one evil System Lord to the other, or risk being destroyed.

Daniel to Apophis: "I know where your son is."

"WHEN I WAS INVITED to direct the episode," says Peter DeLuise, "first off I was reminded of a movie called *Brian's Song*, which was an ode to a football player who is slowly dying. I was moved by the title of the episode, because I realised we were going to help Apophis die.

"Peter Williams had to age over the course of the show, and we used these great leg braces, an idea which I 'borrowed' from the movie *Crash*," DeLuise continues. "I thought I should bind him tight, like Hannibal Lecter, to denote him as a dangerous enemy. Peter Williams, God bless him, had the cataract lenses put over his eyes, he was in old age make-up, he was in a strait-jacket and his legs were bound. He was completely tied down, couldn't move at all. He did a wonderful job of staying Zen-like and never lost his cool. Every time I talked to him I would touch his arm, because I was conscious that I was talking to a blind person who was not used to being blind, which could have been very disconcerting for him."

Whilst that is all very laudable, Peter Williams reveals the director played at least one practical joke on him. "At the very end of the episode, after the last scene was shot, Peter had everyone shut down the cameras, turn out the lights and just walk off the set," Willams recalls. "I was still strapped to the gurney! I lay there calling out, 'Guys?' for several minutes before they came back and let me in on the joke. I still haven't figured out how to pay him back for that one..."

Apophis demands sanctuary.

HOLIDAY

Three men in a body.

The SG-1 team are exploring chambers belonging to Machello, the creator and guardian of a wealth of technology designed to defeat the dreaded Goa'uld. The alien manages to trick Daniel into using a 'body swapping' machine. On their return to Earth, Machello uses Daniel's body to embark on a voyage of discovery. Teal'c and O'Neill bring the machine to Stargate Command, but they accidentally trigger the device, and switch bodies themselves. Machello is finally tracked down, and reveals that his machine's process is irreversible...

Written by:
Tor Alexander Valenza
Directed by:
David Warry-Smith

Guest cast:
Michael Shanks (Machello), Teryl Rothery (Dr Fraiser)

Daniel: "Nice to know you don't just like me for my looks."

MICHAEL SHANKS RECOUNTS HIS memories as Daniel's alter-alter ego. "For a start it was the best episode on paper that I had read for the show. It was very complete from an actor's perspective. Playing both those roles looked as though it was going to be a tough task, but I was really looking forward to it. It was daunting, though," he continues. "I was playing two separate characters (and I do consider Daniel to be a character — he is not me), then having them switch bodies and allowing their two very different personalities to shine through."

Confused? He was! Laughing outright Shanks adds, "You then have to converse with yourself and have them talking to themselves as each other! I looked at the script and thought, 'This is pretty much the hardest thing I've ever had to do...'" Modest about his performance, Shanks thinks "with hindsight, I would have done things a lot differently. It was an opportunity that you rarely get on episodic television and I went for it."

The actor is full of praise for the make-up team: "We had a great prosthetic guy, he deserved an award. Even the head of MGM at the time didn't realise it was me!"

One of Shanks's favourite scenes came at the end, "when I got to play Jack O'Neill for a few shining moments." Asked if he had to study long and hard to get into the part, Shanks reveals with a laugh, "Oh, I think by that point we knew each other well enough to be able to pretty much pull off decent impersonations of one another at any given moment!"

One False Step

Both Jackson and O'Neill are affected by the alien illness.

Written by: Michael Kaplan and John Sanborn
Directed by: William Corcoran

Guest cast: Teryl Rothery (Dr Fraiser), Colin Heath (Technician)

When a UAV crashes during a routine flight on an alien world, SG-1 visits the planet to recover the remote control plane. When members of the alien race start to collapse and fall into a coma-like state, O'Neill and Jackson appear to be suffering adverse effects, too. Acting on a hunch, Carter sets about finding a cure before the illness spreads.

Jackson: "Can you keep an eye on this plant thing for us?"
Teal'c: "I will keep both eyes on it, Daniel Jackson."

"THAT WAS THE EPISODE with the stranger-than-usual costumes and the little huts," recalls producer John Smith. "We shot it out in Stokestead, because it's notoriously drier than the rest of Vancouver. It had to be that way to get an authentic feel to the landscape, especially for the surveillance images where the little plane is flying around photographing the big plants.

"For the costumes we went with a 'mime' look," Smith continues, "the performers looked like basic mime artistes, with the skin suit and white make-up. It turned out pretty good with the whole look of the set, the location, the costumes and the powdered make-up, but we spent the whole time worried that there would be a torrential downpour. We got lucky," laughs Smith. "The gods smiled on us and it stayed dry."

"All the actors and background cast were shaved bald and fitted into a flesh-tone body-suit designed by Christina McQuarrie," make-up supervisor Jan Newman recalls. "The suits had various body markings that were continued onto the hands, feet and faces. Six make-up artists worked on the characters over the six days, each taking about one hour per character."

Teryl Rothery has fond memories of 'One False Step'. "This was the first time anyone saw me go through the Gate. I loved it. Janet steps through the Gate, all five foot two of her, bulked up in a full hazard suit, dwarfed by two burly medical guys. Her first words are, 'Now this is what I call a house call.' It cracks me up."

SHOW AND TELL

O'Neill offers paternal protection to 'Charlie'.

A young boy appears in SGC. The child belongs to a race called the Reetou, and he reveals that his mother has been at SGC for some time, but has remained invisible to human eyes. 'Charlie' has been created in human form to serve as an intermediary between the two races, but a faction of invisible rebel Reetou are also here, intent on destroying all life forms who are potential hosts for the Goa'uld. General Hammond decides it's time to call on the Tok'ra for assistance.

Written by: Jonathan Glassner
Directed by: Peter DeLuise

Guest cast: Teryl Rothery (Dr Fraiser), Carmen Argenziano (Jacob Carter), Jeff Gulka (Charlie)

Teal'c: "If there is a Reetou in this room, it came through the Stargate and it is capable of controlling the iris."

PETER DELUISE SAYS HE'S used to working with kids and animals, or kids and insects as it was in this case. "We used the little boy who plays Gibson Praise in *The X-Files*. He's a lot older than he looks — he was about thirteen." DeLuise laughs, "One of the ways I tried to endear myself to Jeff [Gulka] was by buying him a video game, so that he would know I was 'cool'. But he was way beyond that — he was just getting into girls..."

The director points out his appearance in the episode: "I played the machine gun guard in that one. I've started putting myself in in sneakier ways. You have to look out for various parts of my anatomy now..."

"We gave Peter a shot at directing on *Stargate SG-1* and haven't looked back," comments Jonathan Glassner. "He is so full of energy and loves the show so much that it's great." Brad Wright agrees: "He would come in every five minutes saying, 'I got this great idea!'. Making him creative consultant seemed as good a way as any to get him out of my office and into his own!"

Peter Williams, smiles, "Peter DeLuise is generous with his good fortune. He has this little 'thing' where he will come up and ask you a question about any episode, and if you answer correctly he'll throw you a two-dollar piece. Being struggling actors, of course, we are grateful for all donations. None of the cast ever give it back!"

1969

Sam and Daniel – Far Out and Solid.

Written by:
Brad Wright
Directed by:
Charles Correll

Guest cast:
Alex Zahara (Michael), Aaron Pearl (Lieutenant George Hammond), Amber Rothwell (Jenny), Pamela Perry (Cassandra), Glynis Davies (Catherine), Fred Henderson (Major Thornbird)

A solar flare reconfigures the team's trajectory and they end up back on Earth but in the year 1969. Arrested as spies and later aided by a young George Hammond, who is instructed to help them in the letter written by his older self, the team must locate the Stargate before the next solar flare, or they may be stuck in the past forever.

O'Neill: "We came to Earth to hide among your people a long, long time ago..."
Jackson: "... from a galaxy far, far away."

JUST THE MENTION OF '1969', the episode and the year, brings a smile to Michael Greenburg's face: "I was eighteen in 1969. That episode's amongst my top three or four in the whole series. Brad wrote it. He was only eight in 1969, but he has a great sensibility for the time. It was fun being back in that era, with the Magic Bus, the funky wardrobe and the vibe. The whole cast really bought into it — we just had a blast." Greenburg compliments Jim Menard, the director of photography: "He did a brilliant job. My favourite is the shot in the armoury hall when the crate falls away revealing the Stargate. That was beautifully lit. In film-making terms it really was spectacular."

"It was an out-and-out fun time!" recalls Brad Wright. "After the success of 'Tin Man' in season one, we decided to try for at least one episode every season that's just plain fun. What I love about '1969' is that it doesn't take itself too seriously. One of the things that makes us different from a lot of the other shows on television is our ability to laugh at ourselves, and be a little bit off-beat every now and then. I think most of our audience appreciates that."

If the groovy music wafting SG-1 along the highway sounds particularly cool, it's because it was composed by Bruce Turgon, of the rock band Foreigner. A friend of Michael Greenburg and great fan of the show, Turgon wrote and performed the accompaniment for the 'on the road' part of the episode.

OUT OF MIND

Carter and O'Neill try to elude the Goa'uld.

O'Neill awakens from a cryogenic state to be told he has been frozen for almost eighty years and that the rest of his team is dead. However when he overhears the doctors talking in Goa'uld, he discovers that he and the team are in fact being held in a Goa'uld interrogation stronghold. In command is one of their fiercest enemies – Hathor – who is determined one of the team should be host to her next First Prime.

Story by:
Jonathan Glassner and Brad Wright
Teleplay by:
Jonathan Glassner
Directed by:
Martin Wood

Guest cast:
Teryl Rothery (Dr Fraiser), Suanne Braun (Hathor), Tom Butler (Major General Trofsky), Samantha Ferris (Dr Raully)

O'Neill: "What, the grey doesn't bother you?"

"WHAT'S FUNNY ABOUT 'OUT of Mind' is that none of us particularly liked the character of Hathor," begins Jonathan Glassner. "In fact, Richard Dean Anderson really didn't like her — and it shows." Emphasising that Anderson did like and had great respect for Suanne Braun, who played the goddess, Glassner goes on, "We came up with 'Out Of Mind', but soon realised that in the whole mythology we'd created with the Goa'uld, Hathor was the only one who had a chance of still being out there. So I went up to Rick and said, 'Let me tell you this really cool story,' and he listened and replied, 'Oh that's really cool.' Then I went, 'There's only one catch. The Goa'uld is Hathor.' Rick gave me such a glare but I insisted, 'So what do you think? It's the only way.' He took another couple of seconds before groaning, 'Oh OK! Go ahead.'

"She was an on-going joke between us," Glassner continues. "We'd be having discussions about where to take various ideas and I'd say, 'Come on! I've done some great shows with —' and he'd just look and go, 'Hathor!'" Showing that torture is alive and thriving on the *Stargate* set, Glassner smirks, "There's a website where fans rate their favourite episodes and well into the second season, the highest-rated was always 'Hathor'. So naturally I kept rubbing this in Richard Dean Anderson's face and every so often would pop my head round his door and tease, 'Oh Rick, guess what's number one again this week?' It used to drive him crazy!"

Season Three

Regular Cast:

Richard Dean Anderson (Colonel Jack O'Neill)

Michael Shanks (Dr Daniel Jackson)

Amanda Tapping (Major Samantha Carter)

Christopher Judge (Teal'c)

Don S. Davis (General Hammond)

Teryl Rothery (Dr Janet Fraiser)

Into the Fire

Hammond and Teal'c prepare to thread the needle – Into the Fire.

Written by:
Brad Wright
Directed by:
Martin Wood

Guest cast:
Tony Amendola (Bra'tac), Suanne Braun (Hathor), Tom Butler (Major General Trofsky), Colin Cunningham (Major Davis), Samantha Ferris (Dr Raully), Gary Jones (Technician)

Imprisoned on Hathor's planet, Daniel and Carter are forced to watch O'Neill become a host for the Goa'uld queen's first mate. Back on Earth, General Hammond mounts a rescue attempt of his own. Unaware that a Tok'ra spy has managed to save O'Neill by putting him in a cryogenic chamber, Teal'c and Hammond blast through the Stargate to literally snatch their comrades from the jaws of death...

O'Neill to Jaffa warriors: "Our Beloved Hathor is dead. Well, let's face it! She's a former Queen."

"WHAT I *REALLY* LIKED in that episode," begins director Martin Wood, "was being able to use the 'real' Cheyenne Mountain base set, and then change it just enough so we got a feel of 'is this real or isn't it?' for Hathor's 'duplicate' base. I always thought the huge wall on the base set, that could roll aside and had an equally huge green screen behind it, was so cool. So when Robert Cooper said to me, 'They go in and push a button and the wall starts to move,' I was ecstatic! Remember the scene where they find the power switch to the generator for the 'false' base? That was such a great shot. O'Neill walks into the Gateroom, goes over to a box and says, 'This is new...' Then he pulls the lever and the wall moves aside — I thought it was one of the coolest things I'd ever seen! A lot of fans have said the same thing. Some of them actually thought we'd built a new set just for Hathor to work in, but it was just the same old base."

Wood also reveals that the episode saw the beginning of the force shield that was to play a huge part in the season four story 'Upgrades'. "Touching the shield in 'Into the Fire' was an effect that gave visual effects supervisor James Tichenor a headache. Trying to get this interactive light on the cast, and make it look like there was something between the actors, was a major operation. But one of the things I love most about this show are the practical discussions that we get into over these things."

SETH

Sitting pretty – Seth on his throne.

The team must help Jacob flush a Goa'uld System Lord from hiding. Seth has used alternative religious beliefs, combined with the same biological compound used by Hathor, to maintain a powerful presence on Earth for thousands of years. With agents from the ATF ready to storm the heavily armed fortress at any moment, SG-1 must prevent both Seth's escape and the inevitable bloodshed of his disciples.

Written by:
Jonathan Glassner
Directed by:
William Corcoran

Guest cast:
Carmen Argenziano (Jacob Carter/ Selmak), Robert Duncan (Seth), Mitchell Kosterman (Special Agent James Hamner), Stuart O'Connell (Tommy Levinson)

Daniel: "The men usually became eunuchs."
O'Neill: "Eunuchs! As in snippitty doo-dahs?"

"AS WE WERE GOING to other planets every week, doing a show on our own planet was actually a breath of fresh air," says Jonathan Glassner. "The idea for 'Seth' occurred when I was watching a documentary about David Koresh. I thought, 'What if one of these modern cult leaders actually had powers, or the technology to make it look as though he had powers? How far would he be able to go with that?' Then I realised that as Goa'ulds were able to jump from body to body, they could live for a very long time. Therefore, who's to say that one of them wasn't still around and masquerading as a cult figure? So Seth was sort of a David Koresh metaphor."

Choosing the actor to play the villainous Seth was plain sailing for Glassner: "The curse of casting a bad guy is that everyone always comes in virtually twirling a moustache, your typical bad guy. But Robert Duncan walked in and before he even got into character we all thought he looked kinda scary. We just told him to be himself and he pulled it off."

Amanda Tapping was less than impressed with some aspects of the episode: "We thought the concept was really clever, but I personally feel he should have accomplished so much more than just garner a cult following and a chair." Dissolving into giggles, she snorts, "I mean, where the hell did he get that throne? Did he cart that with him, across the centuries, from Egypt and all through the Galaxy and back through the Stargate and down again? It's a honkin' big throne, c'mon!"

Fair Game

Written by:
Robert C. Cooper
Directed by:
Martin Wood

Guest cast:
Michael David Simms (Secretary of Defence Arthur Simms), Ron Halder (Cronus), Jacqueline Samuda (Nirrti), Vince Crestejo (Yu)

O'Neill's favourite Asgard, Thor, reveals an audacious plan to attack Earth. The tiny alien insists that the Colonel represent the Earth at a meeting with three Goa'uld System Lords – which does not go well. Cronus, the Goa'uld responsible for the death of Teal'c's father, is then found badly beaten, with a slightly less battered Teal'c at his side. A revenge attack on Earth seems likely until Carter manages to use a Goa'uld healing device to restore Cronus to health, and Nirrti's true motivation becomes clear...

Daniel Jackson: "I'll see to the petty needs of the Goa'uld."

DIRECTOR MARTIN WOOD HAS a definite fondness for this episode. "That's where we meet Cronus, Nirrti and Yu," he grins. "We cast the three System Lords with the hope that the story would perhaps turn into another arc. When we were planning the characters it was like, 'OK! What gods are we going to go after?' So we had a raffle, and everybody threw in their three choices. After loads of discussion, we finally came up with three gods who fit the bill. Yu made us laugh a lot. When Yu appeared in the story, we'd be like, 'So — what do you want to do?' and someone would crack, 'What do you mean, what do you want Yu to do? What is it you want Yu to do?' "

According to the director, one of the worst culprits was Richard Dean Anderson. "The only time we got him to behave, if you could call it that, was when he had to do scenes with Thor," says Wood. "Rick had the best time. Each time he walked over to talk to Thor, the puppeteers would make him talk back. There are so many outtakes of Thor yelling things like, 'Dammit! What's my line?' Wood maintains that Adam Behr, the head puppeteer, is a very funny guy, and plays around with the Thor character every chance he gets. One of Wood's major regrets is that there are no crew outtake tapes in wider circulation. "I always print the outtakes, but we're not allowed to let a tape go out to fan conventions or wherever. It's a shame because *Stargate* is the funniest show I've ever worked on, and it just gets funnier every year."

Three of a kind – Yu, Nirrti and Cronus.

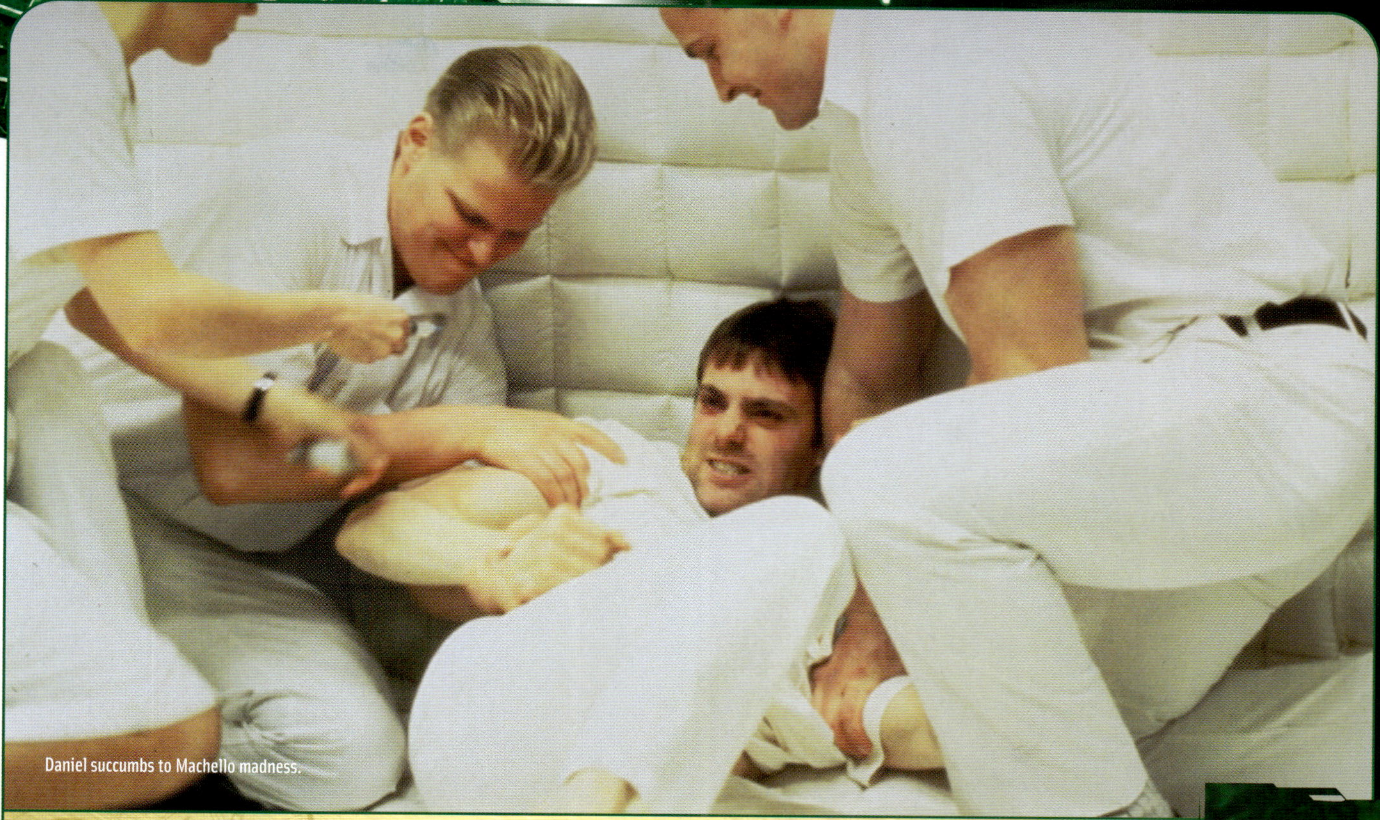

Daniel succumbs to Machello madness.

A routine mission unearths a secret room housing the corpses of the Lindross – a Goa'uld group who challenged the superiority of the System Lords – Daniel is infected with a device designed by Machello to kill Goa'uld. He is diagnosed with schizophrenia. As Teal'c tries to restrain Daniel, the bio-engineered parasite transfers to the Jaffa, with catastrophic effects on his symbiote. When a tablet which Daniel believes could contain the information to cure him is opened, Fraiser and O'Neill are infected too.

Written by: Tor Alexander Valenza
Directed by: Peter DeLuise

Guest cast: Kevin McNulty (Dr Warner), Eric Schneider (Dr McKenzie), Michael Shanks (Machello)

O'Neill: "Let's put up a little sign at the bottom of the ramp saying, 'Gate travel may be hazardous to your health.'"

"THAT EPISODE WAS A great opportunity for Michael Shanks to do his thing," confirms director Peter DeLuise. "It was firmly focused on him and the madness caused by Machello's invention."

Whilst congratulating all involved for acting their socks off, executive producer Jonathan Glassner was not happy with the final scenes: "When we looked at the cut of the last act, when O'Neill, Carter and Fraiser are locked in the science lab and dealing with the worms, we thought it was the most boring thing we'd ever seen! The trouble was, everything that was left in the cut was totally necessary. In desperation, we called the composer, Kevin Kliner. His music transformed the scene to completely on-the-edge-of-your-seat riveting. To me that is the best example of what music can do for a TV show. One day, I'm going to take that example and use it in a class for film students."

Asked how difficult it was to portray a man going quietly mad Richard Dean Anderson replies, with just a trace of a twinkle in his eye, "I have no trouble whatsoever portraying a guy going mad — quietly mad, loudly mad, any sort of mad, primarily because I've been practising that my entire life. I've been, I think, going quietly mad for a very long time. I started when I was a very small boy. So I wasn't taxed at all because I've had lots of practice."

LEARNING CURVE

Student and teacher: but which is which? Carter and Merrin discover together.

Written by:
Heather E. Ash
Directed by:
Martin Wood

Guest cast:
Andrew Airlie (Kalan), Brittney Irvin (Merrin), Lachlan Murdoch (Tomin), Stephanie Shea (Solen), Diane Stapley (Mrs Struble)

Carter and O'Neill discover a smarter-than-average eleven year-old from the planet Orban. Merrin offers to teach Carter how to build a Naquadah reactor. Intent on bringing some fun into the child's life, O'Neill sneaks her into a local school, and the lessons she learns there prove to be infinitely valuable to all the people of Orban.

O'Neill: "Teal'c's eager on the inside."

WRITER HEATHER E. ASH REVEALS: "This was the script that got me hired to join the full-time writing staff. My draft was distributed to the crew without a rewrite by Brad or Jonathan, which was a first for a freelance script (and the last time it happened for me). I was so impressed with both Rick and Christopher Judge, and their interaction with the children. Especially the scene where Merrin leaves for the last time, and O'Neill is watching her go. I got teary watching it."

Amanda Tapping reveals a fun moment for Carter and Merrin: "There's a scene in the lab where we get that energy wave off the bomb. Without telling us, the crew rigged up a bunch of vibrating devices onto the big metal desk. So when the bomb exploded, the table actually shook. The reaction you see on screen really is us going, 'Argh! My God!' I just love it when the crew do little things like that."

Tapping particularly enjoyed the episode, she says, "because of the moral dilemma it posed, as in, 'Do we have the right to get that involved in another people's way of life?' It's a question we ask often on *Stargate* but I found it really poignant that the children are essentially put out to pasture. There's got to be more you can teach them. When Merrin insists she wants the nanocytes which make her so intelligent removed, which will effectively turn her into a vegetable, and I tell her that most of the best things in my life happened after I was fifteen. I changed the line to include my personal observation as Amanda, and they kept it in. I loved the way that scene played."

Point of View

A second Dr Carter, accompanied by a very live and kicking Major Kawalsky, slips through the quantum mirror into Area 51. Identical to SG-1's Carter except for her longer hair and the fact that she's a civilian, the new Sam reveals she was married to O'Neill, before his demise at the hands of the Goa'uld. Gamely resisting all advances from 'Mrs' O'Neill, the Colonel works with the rest of SG-1 to help both Carters find a way to return to their own reality.

Story by:
Jonathan Glassner, Brad Wright, Robert C. Cooper, Tor Alexander Valenza
Teleplay by:
Jonathan Glassner and Brad Wright
Directed by:
Peter DeLuise

Guest Cast:
Jay Acovone (Major Charles Kawalsky), Peter Williams (Apophis), Ty Olsson (Jaffa #1), Shawn Reis (Jaffa #2), Tracy Westerholm (SF Guard)

O'Neill to Dr Carter: "How could you marry such a loser?"

"'**POINT OF VIEW' CAME** about because we wanted Carter and O'Neill to kiss," admits Jonathan Glassner. "In the original script, the alternative reality Carter was also an officer, but our Air Force advisors refused to grant permission for that. Their official stance was: 'Two military officers cannot kiss.' Even when I said, 'How do you know that's the rule in an alternate reality?' they said it didn't matter. So Brad and I asked how it would be if one wasn't in the military, and they let us do that."

Jovial Peter DeLuise concentrates on the most difficult challenge: the issue of the twin Carters' coiffure: "As you know, hair, in production, is one of the bigger considerations for women, and Amanda was required to do half of each scene with her photo double, go off and change, then come back and do the next half. Her hair took about half an hour to change over because if she had the wig on we'd do the first version and then we would have to make her real hair all nice and presentable so she didn't have 'wig head'."

DeLuise is justifiably proud of pulling off the scene in the medical centre when Carter had to hold her own hand. "Usually you can't touch your other self without it looking fake," he admits. "But our audience is quite savvy and knows that if you take a really close look at that scene the seam is flawless, and that's because where her hands touch is not where the seam is. It's down near the elbow where the blanket is covering her up." So now we know.

It's Hammond and Teal'c, but not as we know them.

Deadman's Switch

Behold! The bounty hunter Aris Boch.

Written by:
Robert C. Cooper
Directed by:
Martin Wood

Guest Cast:
Sam J. Jones (Aris Boch), Mark Holden (Korra)

On planet PJ6-877 SG-1 are captured by intergalactic bounty hunter Aris Boch. Painfully addicted to a substance he can only get from the Goa'uld, Boch offers to trade the lives of SG-1 for that of a criminal named Kel'tar – so long as they assist in his capture. When they realise the criminal is in fact Korra, a Tok'ra, and therefore an ally, SG-1 must find a way to convince their captor to let them go.

O'Neill: "We're exactly one zat gun short of actually having a zat gun."

MARTIN WOOD STRUGGLES TO stop laughing when reminiscing about 'Deadman's Switch': "For a start, it's the first one that doesn't actually have a Stargate in it. Michael Greenburg turned to us one day and said, 'You know what? There's no Stargate in this episode of *Stargate*. We should rename the show — *Stargate (or not)*!'"

Wood also recalls, "Sam Jones was hilarious. One of his lines was, 'My wife and son were kidnapped!' I said to him, 'Sam, you don't actually have a wife.' He said, 'What do you mean? I thought I did.' So I explained that it was just Aris Boch bluffing. So Sam went, 'OK — but how would you say this line?' I gave him a reading, which he repeated exactly, I shot it, and on we went. The whole episode was like that with him. I think Sam really is an alien. He doesn't understand the rules and regulations of human life, so brought this alien character to life in a way that nobody else could."

Wood's favourite part was when the bounty hunter's ship, his Teltac, climbs up over the rise: "I fought for that shot. I loved it so much. I took the idea from the movie *Blue Thunder*, when the helicopter is revealed."

Wood recalls the skills displayed by Christopher Judge: "When you see Teal'c throw the smoke bomb into the cave, the very first time he threw it, it landed in the cave, exactly as it was supposed to. I can't throw that far when I'm standing up and looking, but Chris was lying down and he just lobbed this thing. Sadly we couldn't use the shot because when he opened up the smoke bomb he burned his thumb, and then ruined the take by yelling some very unsavoury words!"

A medieval native takes the restraining order very seriously.

Arriving at a medieval village, Daniel Jackson releases a young girl who is tied to a stake, whilst O'Neill recognises that the marks on her body are chicken pox, rather than the manifestation of an evil presence. Less than impressed, the local Canon proclaims that SG-1 are agents of the Devil. With the team offered up as sacrifices to the Unas that haunts the community, it's left to the very devout Simon to go against all he believes in order to free SG-1.

Written by: Carl Binder
Directed by: Peter DeLuise

Guest cast: David McNally (Simon), Alan C. Peterson (Canon), Laura Mennell (Mary), Richard Morwich (Unas), John R. Taylor (Elder), Christopher Judge (Voice of the Unas)

Teal'c: "Have you not read the Bible, O'Neill?"
O'Neill: "Not all of it. Actually, I'm listening to it on tape. Don't tell me how it ends."

AMANDA TAPPING REMEMBERS, "PETER DeLuise, who makes everything fun, directed it. He had crewmembers dressed up as villagers playing havoc. The village set was phenomenal. That was one of my favourite sets ever for attention to detail. You know how the villagers chained us to metal hooks? Well, there was actual rust going down the walls from the metal. Also the set crew had moss growing up some of the walls, too — the sort of detail that you maybe don't see straight-off when you're watching the episode, but if you're acting in that kind of environment, it's just amazing."

Christopher Judge recalls: "When I first read it, and got to the part where Teal'c gets thrown down into the water, I just wanted to make sure that it wasn't going to be me doing it!" Ignoring the fact that he was a professionally trained athlete, Judge says, "I'm not the strongest swimmer in the world, plus I knew that water would be freezing. So I was extremely happy that I had a stunt double for it. He certainly earned his money."

Judge adds, "Peter directed it, so it was a hoot to do. He didn't tell the women who were watching over my body that I would be coming back to life. The shock on their faces was genuine, they were scared silly! It was the first time we had re-visited the Unas, and Alan Peterson who played the Canon went wonderfully over the top with his delivery, and had us all falling about."

Production Design

Richard Hudolin: "On most television shows, it's all about offices and police cars. On this show we don't do offices — we do worlds."

Asked where he gets the inspiration to create the award-winning designs for *Stargate SG-1*, production design master Richard Hudolin shrugs and says, "It's what we do! The writers present us with a situation and we come up with a look, or a feel, or a style. Then we make sure we know how to do it, and that we have the right people to get it done. I have a first class crew and know that any one of them can deliver the product without me having to worry about it." Insisting that the process is a collaborative affair, Hudolin whole-heartedly endorses the efforts of his team: "We have seven people in the art department, headed up by Bridget McGuire. Thom Wells heads construction, then there's the set decorators and props people all involved in making it happen. I do assign specific tasks, but we have an open art department so we all take a look at what other people are up to and help each other. Often people from other parts of production will wander in and offer their comments. Its one of the things I love about this job."

Above: Production design art for 'Red Sky'.

Opposite top: Production design art for the Nox's Cloud City.

Opposite bottom: Production design art for Drey'ac and Fro'tak's home in 'Family'.

Hudolin claims he never gets nervous because there is simply no time. "I get the themes for ten shows well in advance," he explains, "so I'm working on this way ahead of everyone else." By the time an episode is actually being shot, Hudolin has long moved on, and is deep in preparation for the next batch. "If I go on set when they're shooting, I don't know what the heck is going on!" he laughs, but the designer maintains that employing a selective memory is one of the tools that keeps his mind fresh for the next project. "As soon as the shooting crew gets there I totally erase everything about that show from my mind. I can't remember a thing unless someone tells me what sets were involved. I just know that everything we do is great, and that's good enough for me." When pushed, Hudolin does consider 'The Nox', 'Spirits', 'Show and Tell', 'Thor's Chariot' and 'Family' as some of the most memorable episodes from the first two seasons. "You know, we won a Gemini award," he says proudly, "but when I was first asked to put an episode in for consideration, I had to look at the tapes to decide which one to nominate because it all becomes such a blur." He grins, "I couldn't look to the future if I kept looking back at the others."

Whilst there may be the odd blooper (not many, we're assured) that occurs when an episode is being shot, Hudolin is adamant that no such thing ever happens during the design and construction process, teasing, "There's been none that I'm going to tell you about! Actually, because we move so quickly, you have to pick up potential

errors straight away. I'll be walking by a set and if I don't catch something when somebody is starting to do it, it can lead to some pretty ugly pieces of work. They all laugh at me because I have this thing about rocks. Making rocks and caves is really difficult and you have to work at it and think about what you're doing, but every now and then I'll get on this rant and I'll be walking by a set and go, 'What the hell is that cartoon rock? Are the Flintstones working here?' The crew just watch me light up. Sometimes they do it deliberately just to get me riled. They enjoy watching me rant." It must be because raised voices are such an unusual occurrence. "You don't get much of that on our set," Hudolin confirms. "It doesn't achieve anything. No one on our set would pay attention anyway."

There is one piece of construction of which Hudolin is extremely proud. "We have a portable Stargate, which we take on location. It's an exact copy of the one in the studio, except the inner ring doesn't move. It takes six guys about a day to set it up because it has to be done in a very specific way, but it's a beautiful piece of engineering."

This engineering skill came to the fore many times during season one. "That first year it rained till about June and we'd go on location and have to build roads because the trucks would sink into the ground," Hudolin recalls. Things were a lot more palatable for the crew in season two, however. "That was a great year, because we had established our rhythm and our systems. That made it all great fun."

According to Hudolin, the team slogan is "Scripts? We don't need no stinkin' scripts!" coined because work on the complicated structures is always well underway before a single line of dialogue is committed to paper. "You must understand that when we begin the process of designing a set, we don't have anything as formal as a script," he explains. "How it starts is we'll be talking with Robert Cooper or Brad Wright, and, taking the

Paul Mullie: "I'm amazed that I can visualise a scene in my head when I'm writing it, and Richard and his team deliver more or less the exact same thing."

Below: Production drawing of Hell, from 'Jolinar's Memories'/'The Devil You Know'.

'The Curse' as an example, they'll say something like 'We've got to go into a tomb!' My colleague Doug McLean and I will ask, 'Well, what sort of tomb? How many rooms? How many hallways? What happens in this tomb?' At that point they'll usually admit that they haven't exactly written anything yet, but they'd like some special little touches — a sarcophagus here, a sliding wall there. Nothing too challenging, you understand!

"The challenge comes from trying to re-visit existing sets and materials without our audience realising we're doing it," Hudolin continues. "The nature of *Stargate* is that we're constantly trying to produce movie-quality sets on a television budget, so anything we can recycle is used to the max." Whilst it may seem that such a frugal attitude toward film production is laudable, Hudolin yells, "Are you kidding? Doug and I often just scratch our heads and think, 'What the hell are we going to do with this now? This is its third use!'" A typical example is the cargo ship built for 'Deadman's Switch'. "We were only supposed to use that thing once," confides Doug McLean, "but we ended up using it about fourteen times."

One of the biggest tests to the production team's ingenuity was the main set for 'Jolinar's Memories'/'The Devil You Know'. "It was supposed to be a representation of Hell," grins Hudolin, "but I just call it Hell." Colleague McLean claims, "It wasn't that bad. Certainly it was one of our biggest ventures. It took over sound stage six — which in itself is massive — and we would have built more but we ran out of space and money! It was a lot of fun though, because we wound up re-using lots of bits from old shows. Much of the texture on the walls came out of the mud huts we built for 'One False Step'. They were whitewashed domes on the outside, but foam on the inside, and we'd kept them for ages trying to figure out a use for them. We ended up breaking them apart, flattening them out and using the inside as the basis for the textural structure of Hell."

The production team's relationship with the show's writers and producers continues to improve as the series progresses. "You know, we've never started something and had them come back and tell us it doesn't correspond

Below: Design for the indoor village set in 'Demons'.

Right: Concept drawings for Osiris's ship in 'The Curse'.

Opposite top: Another indoor 'outdoor' set, the garden from 'Maternal Instinct'.

Opposite below left: Production design art for the meeting house in 'Spirits'.

Opposite below right: Production design for the bounty hunter's ship in 'Deadman's Switch'.

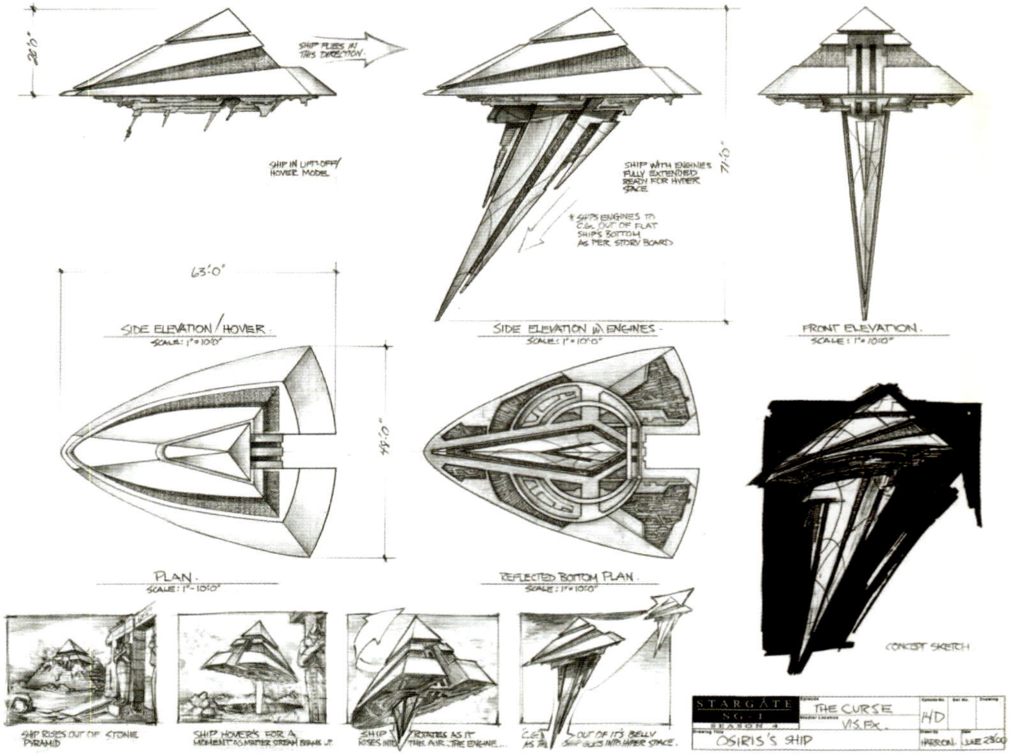

to what they've written," McLean points out proudly. "In practice, they actually write to what we're designing. They are pretty good that way. Of course, it happens occasionally that in the process — as we're designing — one of them will come down and go, 'Yeah! That's prefect. Great! Now he goes out this door...' and we'll go, 'Door? What door? You didn't mention a door the last time we spoke!' And their response will be, 'Oh yeah! We need doors at both ends, sorry.'" Hudolin swears that he and his team are nothing if not patient. "It's the good relationship that saves them a lot of the time, because when we go back to the writers and tell them we can do what they want but it will cost a certain amount, they'll look at our designs and go, 'Wow! This is great. We need to use that set more.' Often they will increase the size of a scene to accommodate what we've created."

One of the favourite sets amongst cast and crew is the village set created for 'Demons'. "That was the first time we'd actually tried what's called an interior for exterior set," McLean reveals. "I wondered what would happen if we used the existing studio space instead of going on location. 'Demons' was another example of the crew getting thoroughly immersed and adding little touches that wouldn't be immediately apparent to the viewers at home."

The team is duly proud of the episode 'Maternal Instinct' too. Hudolin says, "Those sets work so well because we combined them with the visual effects. There are one or two big shots where you have matte painting and the set combined on the screen, and you're convinced that you are really looking at the sky. We also build the set on panels, and we dropped one panel down so that Jim Menard, the director of photography, could light it from one source — like a sun shining — which made the whole thing look totally realistic."

Asked if there's ever been an occasion when they've been given a brief that sounded too far outside the realms of possibility, Hudolin answers with an unequivocal "No! Not in five years. Our guys live up to that old saying: 'We can do the impossible. Miracles take a little longer...'"

STARGATE
SG-1
SEASON 3
Episode
MATERNAL INSTINCT
Episode No.
20C
Set No.
Drawing
Studio/ Location
Drawing Title
TEMPLE COURTYARD GARDENS.
Drawn by
HARRON
Date
SEPT. 03/99

REVISED
STARGATE
SG·1
SEASON 2
Drawing Title
EXT. VILLAGE
& LONGHOUSE
"SPIRITS" 14/07/98
Episode #
13
Set No.
06
Drawing
2

STARGATE
SG·1
INT. GOA'ULD CARGO SHIP "COCKPIT"
NRCD STAGE 3
DEAD MAN SWITCH
7C

Rules of Engagement

Written by:
Terry Curtis Fox
Directed by:
William F. Gereghty

Guest cast:
Peter Williams (Apophis), Aaron Craven (Captain Kyle Rogers), Dion Johnstone (Captain Nelson), Jesse Moss (Lt J. Hibbard)

The team step through the gate straight into a pitched battle between SG forces and a group of Jaffa. Waking inside a prison tent SG-1 discover a group of young men intent on fulfilling their standing orders, which were to practice non-lethal war games in readiness for the invasion of Earth. The team dupe the soldiers into believing that Teal'c is still Apophis's First in order to persuade them to surrender.

Teal'c to Jaffa troops: "This is Colonel O'Neill. He is much loved by Apophis."

"ONE OF THE VERY best things about 'Rules of Engagement' was that it gave me a chance romp around like a kid again," chuckles Christopher Judge. "We did a lot of fighting with Rick and that's his thing, rolling around in the mud and all that action stuff. Because he literally threw himself into it, so did everyone else. I remember one day when it was raining and we had to do a lot of running and diving in the dirt, Rick and I just turned to each other and said, 'This is the best day we've had all season!'" Judge grins, "We were these two old guys who were now back to being kids again." Judge says the humorous banter between Teal'c and O'Neill carried on off-camera too. "We had a really good time when the cameras stopped rolling and kind of kept the Teal'c/O'Neill master/servant thing going. I think it's the only time Richard Dean Anderson served me lunch. Ah! Only kidding folks."

Very often the episode we see on television is very different to what was first proposed. "'Rules of Engagement' was a script that went through three incarnations," explains Brad Wright. "The first, written by Terry Curtis Fox, bears almost no resemblance to what was finally committed to film. Our story editor at the time, Tor Valenza, came up with a spin on Terry's story that finally made it work for me — the idea of young soldiers training to infiltrate the Tauri and being left behind. I then did a very heavy re-write on Tor's script and that's what we shot."

Apophis's First Prime inspects the troops.

Forever in a Day

Sha're and Daniel, alone at last.

Teal'c makes the decision to kill Ammonet, the Goa'uld infesting Daniel's wife Sha're, rather than let her destroy him. Unable to forgive Teal'c for his actions nor continue his quest through the Stargate without Sha're as his goal, Daniel rejects Teal'c's friendship, resigns from the Stargate programme and leaves. However, the gods and Sha're still have plans in store which mean Daniel must overcome his grief and forgive Teal'c before he can go on to fulfil a promise.

Written by:
Jonathan Glassner
Directed by:
Peter DeLuise

Guest cast:
Erick Avari (Kasuf), Vaitiare Bandera (Sha're/Ammonet), Jason Schombing (Robert Rothman)

Daniel Jackson: "The SGC may be the single most important endeavour for the future of Mankind."

JONATHAN GLASSNER THINKS THIS was his best script for the series: "The idea came out of a desire to finally wrap up the Sha're story. However, Sha're being out there was Daniel Jackson's over-riding motivation to stay with SG-1, so we had to come up with a new goal. That's where Robert Cooper's idea for the Harsesis child came in."

'Forever in a Day' is one of Michael Shanks's favourites too: "It marked the end of a storyline that was very significant to Daniel, and as such was a very emotional time for me. It was a lot of fun to play the sadness and to explore the torn nature of the decisions he was making." Shanks agrees with Wright that "the 'funeral' scene and the scenes in the apartment were wonderful. Those were rare opportunities to go to personal places. *Stargate* being steeped in the science fiction mode, it was a treat to take Daniel on this deeply personal journey and have him pop up on the other side."

Shanks also notes: "It was done with my girlfriend at the time, Vaitiare Bandera, and it held a lot of personal angst, but the bedroom scene was completely natural, except there were all these people standing around with cameras. Vaitiare was very nervous and much more reserved because she wasn't as comfortable with the crew as I was. It felt odd in my own mind because I kept thinking, 'This is us as we usually are. We do this all the time. Go film something interesting!'"

PAST & PRESENT

A difficult decision has to be made. Hammond and O'Neill in grim mood.

Written by:
Tor Alexander Valenza
Directed by:
William F. Gereghty

Guest cast:
Megan Leitch (Ke'ra), Marya Delver (Layale), Jason Gray-Stanford (Orner), Luisa Cianni (Woman)

Faced with a population who appear to be suffering from mass amnesia caused by an apocalyptic event they call the 'Vorlix', SG-1 encounter a young woman named Ke'ra, who seems to hold some of the clues as to what happened. Whilst she works with Fraiser and Carter to find a cure for what ails her people, Ke'ra and Daniel discover a mutual attraction...

O'Neill: "Oh My! There's a distinct lack of optimism in this room."

"THIS EPISODE GIVES A little insight into Daniel's nicer side," smiles Michael Shanks. "It was interesting from a 'Daniel defending the villain' perspective. It wasn't typical, so it was important for me to realise that all the things he appeared to be doing out of petulance weren't so much 'whiny' as they were noble."

The actor gives due credit to Brad Wright who, he insists, "did a very good job of making sure that Daniel was properly motivated, and that the other characters were encouraged into acting in more of a protective way. They were more or less saying to Daniel, 'You may be going through what you're going through, and we'll watch you going through it because we can see your point of view, but at the same time we can't let you be so naïve. We have to watch your back.' I think that led to a very real dynamic between the characters and the situation. I know it certainly helped me play it."

One thing Shanks wasn't so pleased with was the order of play. "It was very odd because that episode came right after 'Forever in a Day'. We were actually meant to film 'Past & Present' a few weeks before 'Forever in a Day', but the script needed some adjustments, so it kept getting put back. It was just the luck of the draw that in the episode immediately after Daniel's wife dies, he decides to make out with another girl! That situation never quite sat right with me, even though I do know that that is just the way television works."

Jolinar's Memories

Devlishly clever Sokar.

Martouf brings news that Carter's father has been taken prisoner by the System Lord Sokar. The Goa'uld has turned a small moon, Netu, into a living Hell. Determined to rescue Jacob/Selmak's body, or at the very least escape with knowledge vital to the survival of the Tok'ra, Martouf asks Sam to access the memories of his dead wife Jolinar – believed to be the only person ever to have left Netu alive.

Written by:
Sonny Wareham and Daniel Stashower
Directed by:
Peter DeLuise

Guest cast:
Carmen Argenziano (Jacob Carter/Selmak), JR Bourne (Martouf), William de Vry (Aldwin), Bob Dawson (Bynarr), Dion Johnstone (Na'onak), Peter Williams (Apophis), David Palffy (Sokar), Tanya Reid (Jolinar)

Martouf: "Shall we embark?"
O'Neill: "By all means. To Hell with us."

JONATHAN GLASSNER BEGINS, "IT was the largest set I've ever seen. The reason this episode became a two-parter was simply because we couldn't afford to do it as a stand-alone piece. It was almost as expensive as the pilot. Robert Cooper, genius that he is, came up with another script which became 'The Devil You Know', and we merged the two budgets together to pay for the whole shebang. It took the crew a couple of months to build the set and we shot it all as one episode."

Amanda Tapping agrees the episodes were big in many ways: "First because I always love episodes with Jacob in them and with Martouf. Then, of course, there was that amazing set. Four storeys of Hell! It was dirty. It was hot. Then there was all the turmoil you could see us going through physically and emotionally."

Director Peter DeLuise remembers the efforts taken by director of photography Peter Woeste to get just the right look for the flashback sequences. DeLuise refers to it as "the smeary dreams". Elaborating he says, "'Smeary dreams' is when you shoot at six frames a second, instead of twenty-four. What happens is each frame of film is duplicated many times, and, as there is movement, you get a smear. It looks like the residual image of your hand in its first, second, third, fourth position — all in one go. It gives a little bit of a strobing/smearing effect."

THE DEVIL YOU KNOW

Apophis shows off his new look.

Written by:
Robert C. Cooper
Directed by:
Peter DeLuise

Guest cast:
Carmen Argenziano (Jacob Carter/ Selmak), JR Bourne (Martouf), William de Vry (Aldwin), Bob Dawson (Bynarr), Peter Williams (Apophis), Dion Johnstone (Na'onak), David Palffy (Sokar), Tanya Reid (Jolinar)

The attempt to rescue Jacob Carter ends with O'Neill, Carter, Daniel and Martouf being captured by Apophis. Aware that the original rescue attempt has failed, the Tok'ra deliver a bomb they insist must be used to destroy the moon, its inhabitants and all nearby ships. Teal'c must rely on his knowledge of Apophis's modus operandi to pluck his friends to safety.

O'Neill: "They gave me something that reminded me of the seventies."

WRITER ROBERT COOPER CONFIRMS that this episode really came about because of economics: "A team of writers had pitched what eventually became part one. We liked the idea because it involved a rescue mission to save Jacob, and explored the consequences of Jacob becoming a Tok'ra host. We hooked into the concept he had been sent to the Goa'uld version of Hell. When the script came in, we realised that we couldn't afford to build the set that was the centrepiece for the episode. So, 'The Devil You Know' was born. In the end all the scrambling was worth it, not least because the set was so magnificent it won a well-deserved Gemini for our talented production design team!"

Robert Cooper continues by revealing, "Some people have wondered why we created this really cool Goa'uld in Sokar, only to kill him off right away. Well, we originally killed Apophis because we had beaten him so many times that he was no longer scary. Then we realised we could bring him back in dramatic fashion, having him take over the realm of the scariest Goa'uld we could think of. We built Sokar up because the more powerful he was, the more powerful Apophis would become when he defeated him."

Commenting on the great manicure sported by Sokar, Peter DeLuise says, "The nails were inspired Robert DeNiro's character in *Angel Heart*. Sokar's eyes were an homage to Darth Maul in *The Phantom Menace*, and the albino look and the hood were from the classic evil Emperor, that Ian McDairmid played in *Return of the Jedi*."

The arrival of some unwelcome visitors.

A group of aliens manage to infiltrate the SGC by taking on the looks and personality of the personnel. The SG-1 team is knocked unconscious by a sedative administered by a bogus Janet Fraiser. Teal'c awakes and realises the situation. He manages to hold the hostile visitors at bay whilst Carter escapes and informs Colonel Maybourne of the 'Foothold' crisis. Taken in by two creatures purporting to be O'Neill and Daniel Jackson, Maybourne persuades Carter to return with him.

Written by: Heather E. Ash
Directed by: Andy Mikita

Guest cast: Tom McBeath (Colonel Harry Maybourne), Colin Cunningham (Major Davis), Richard Leacock (Colonel Brogen), Colin Lawrence (Sergeant Warren), Dan Shea (Sergeant Siler)

Carter: "Maybourne, you are an idiot every day of the week. Why couldn't you have taken one day off?"

WRITER HEATHER ASH ADMITS, "This was an extremely hard script to write. We spent a lot of time trying to figure it out. Once we'd settled on the 'invasion' model, we had to decide where Carter would go for help. Originally, she sought Major Davis's help. Later, we decided it would be more compelling to have her join with Colonel Maybourne, the one person she couldn't trust."

"When we cast Tom as Maybourne," Jonathan Glassner begins , "like Robert Duncan in 'Seth', most of the people that came in were these big, mean-looking guys. Tom is this scrawny guy who is the most gentle person. Having him act against type and letting him have fun with it actually worked out very well."

Amanda Tapping concurs, "Tom McBeath is an amazing actor and a really wonderful guy, so it's very hard to hate him." Tapping also felt the episode gave her "the chance to show that dichotomy of not trusting. Carter — who does everything by the book — suddenly turns her back saying, 'Nah! I don't trust you guys.'" The actress has particularly fond memories of the scene in the café: "I came up with the 'Maybourne, you're an idiot every day of the week. Why couldn't you have taken one day off?' line." Thrilled she yells, "That was me! I was looking at one of the fan websites which talks about favourite *SG-1* lines and there it was! When I saw that, it was like one of those 'Woohoo' moments."

Teal'c

Teal'c: "In my world, I would be well within my rights to dismember you."

Habitually late, prone to fits of giggling and a firm believer that bashing a little ball about with a metal pole is a commendable sport (he's a keen golfer) — Christopher Judge possesses more than a few personal foibles the sombre Teal'c would find hard to understand. As chief protector and second-in-command to the System Lord Apophis, the stoic Jaffa executed many difficult and unpleasant tasks, not to mention executing innocent aliens into the bargain. Judge says that in real life it's his colleagues who have to display fortitude and patience. "To tell you the truth, I don't know how the guys at *SG-1* put up with me," he laughs. Fortunately, the actor's co-stars and colleagues cope remarkably well. Make-up supervisor Jan Newman describes Judge as the bane of her life, yet the normally genteel lady chuckles, "I have no compunction about shouting like a fishwife when he's kept us waiting. But he is so adorable that he can be an hour late and within three seconds I've forgiven him." Judge thinks it's a pity Apophis doesn't feel the same way. Producer John Smith grins, "Christopher will eventually come in with a big smile on his face and push everybody — in a very gentle way, not hard enough to knock us over as he's a big guy — but it tickles him to do it and it makes us laugh."

However, the actor maintains it's everyone else that keeps him laughing, protesting, "Amanda Tapping can break my composure with one look." Judge's exuberance extends to the other members of the cast, particularly Michael Shanks with whom he has forged a firm friendship. "I'm always teasing Shanks about the way he prepares for every scene," laughs Judge. "Me? I just ask him if I need to read the script."

Speaking socially as well as professionally, Judge claims, "Shanks and I are as different as chalk and cheese. He's a quiet, country boy at heart and I'm a city slicker, but we gelled straight off and have stayed that way." As well as joining the other sporty cast members in a love of skiing, Judge says Michael Shanks and Richard Dean Anderson share his fascination with golf. In a fit of uncharacteristic modesty he admits, "I'm not as good as they are yet, but I'm working on it. In fact, if I'm not hanging out on the set or spending time with my kids, you'll most likely find me practising my swing on the golf course."

Not that it's all play and no work for the ex-First Prime of Apophis, Serpent God. Since his initial stiff-upper-lip appearances, SG-1's tower of strength and authority on all things Goa'uld has been loosening up a little.

"I spoke with the writers about how Teal'c was starting to assimilate, and brought it to their attention that he has a great sense of humour," Judge recalls. "It's just different from a human sense of humour. I wanted to make a conscious effort to get Teal'c to make what he thought were jokes and to bring out the human characteristics he has that had so far been dormant in the show." Teal'c's slant on the 'wild horses couldn't drag me away' promise in 'Message in a Bottle' being a prime example. In the episode, an alien device grows robotic legs and pins SG-1's team leader to the wall. As the temperature rises unbearably within the Gateroom, and death becomes a distinct possibility, O'Neill asks Teal'c to leave. The Jaffa replies, "Undomesticated equines could not force me to leave." O'Neill starts to point out what his friend should have said before he realises that, yes, Teal'c has made a joke...

Christopher Judge was born and raised in Los Angeles where, he jokes, "the closest I came to any wild life was in the bars." The jovial ex-All American footballer was drawn to acting from an early age. "I studied Telecommunications and Film at the University of Oregon, and knew I was destined to be in the spotlight," he says. Judge's 'break' came when he won a competition, which earned him a job as morning DJ on a West Coast radio station. From there it was a hop, skip and a jump to television, where he appeared *in The Fresh Prince of Bel Air* and *21 Jump Street* (alongside Peter DeLuise). As well as appearing in a wealth of motion pictures, including *Bird on a Wire* with Mel Gibson and Goldie Hawn and *House Party II*, Judge also cut his teeth behind the scenes when he produced a short film entitled *Hacks*, a career extension he intends to pursue alongside his *Stargate SG-1* stint. Known amongst his friends as "the Barry White of SG-1" Judge has recorded a CD featuring many of his favourite types of musical styles

A man of many talents, Judge has been known to wax lyrical about the role of black actors in mainstream productions. "When I initially glanced at the script for *Stargate SG-1*, I thought this was going to be yet another example of where the big, tough, black guy is your stereotyped reformed slave," he recalls. "But when I read it properly, I realised that here was a chance to let 'the guy with the muscle' be the one who might just lead his people from slavery — that there was a nobility in him." Catching himself, Judge goes on, "Of course, he can't do that without some sex. That's one of the reasons Teal'c doesn't smile so much. His wife is hidden on another planet!"

Teal'c: "If I were still loyal to the Goa'uld you would know it. It would be immediately apparent, as I would not hesitate to kill you where you sit."

Talking with Judge is akin to riding a rollercoaster. He can be as deep and serious as they come one moment, ridiculously silly the next. It's a notion the actor is keen to foster in his performance of the quiet Jaffa. "As a character I didn't have a lot to say in the beginning, which I felt was in keeping with how he was meant to be," he says. "My reactions as Teal'c were more honest in that they were pertinent to an intelligent man who finds himself in an unfamiliar environment on an unknown world. As the series progresses and Teal'c does speak, it's because he really has something to say worth hearing. He's more interactive with his companions and in tune with those around him."

Until season three, Earth's strong and silent resident alien, Teal'c, could be relied upon to face every challenge presented to SG-1 with calm stoicism and nothing more than a well-timed lift of a brow. How things have changed. Christopher Judge is delighted the Jaffa's true personality was allowed to come to the fore in the show's middle seasons. "To be honest I was getting a little tired of keeping the stony face," grins Judge, "especially when it's the complete antithesis of my own, shall we say, ebullient nature. I mean, four years down the line, it would have appeared strange had Teal'c not started to display some of his latent human attributes. He is from human stock. It stands to reason that, removed from constant exposure to the stronger elements of the Goa'uld, he would revert to type at some time or other, and begin to show the more acceptable side of his make-up."

With an inherent sense of the ridiculous and a predisposition towards wicked behaviour, it's no wonder Judge struggles to keep a straight face during some of the more frivolous episodes of the show. "If you watch 'Urgo'," he chuckles, "you'll see that there are hardly any shots of Teal'c. That's because there were very few where I'm not

doubled over with laughter! Dom DeLuise is a very funny man and to watch his son Peter encouraging his dad's outrageous behaviour was, in itself, hilarious."

Outstanding guest stars aside, Judge admits that any of his co-stars can reduce him to a helpless state: "Richard Dean Anderson has one of the most wicked senses of humour known to man, and I'm not even going to try to describe how duplicitous and down right sneaky Michael Shanks can be when he wants to!" Judge has never forgiven Shanks for terrifying the life out of him by pretending there was a bear in the woods whilst they were shooting an early episode of the show. "There was some sort of payback in season four though," Judge says, "when a bear actually did wander into frame while Shanks was shooting a scene for 'Scorched Earth'. The shoe was definitely on the other foot then! Of course, I had some important business to attend to in my trailer, so had to remove myself from the scene and wasn't around to tease him that much." Nothing to do with being scared of the bear, then.

That said, by seasons three and four Teal'c is definitely becoming more comfortable as a part of the team. "He's really participating more by offering his input," Judge agrees, "rather than just following O'Neill into battle. In 'Scorched Earth', for instance, O'Neill asks why he didn't try to stop Daniel from going back to the 'enemy' ship, and Teal'c says it's because he didn't entirely disagree with what Daniel was trying to do. It was one of those times where we see that Teal'c does now feel comfortable enough to offer a direct challenge. I think that's because he stopped feeling like an outsider, and really feels like part of the team rather than just the muscle who helps beat up the bad guys when needed. His relationship with everyone in SG-1, and Jack O'Neill in particular, has really warmed up. I loved it when we did all the crazy stuff in 'Window of Opportunity', like the golf and the juggling, and supporting each other when we were regurgitating Carter's technobabble or correcting Daniel's linguistic translations. The understated bond between Teal'c and O'Neill was fun to do."

The Jaffa's relationships with members of his own race have been given more attention, too. "It's a development which pleases me greatly," smirks Judge. "In 'Crossroads' we actually see him involved in a relationship with a woman from his past, and the depth of emotion he displays takes everyone by surprise. Not just in that episode, but later on when his determination to get Tanith puts both Teal'c and O'Neill in peril. I'm grateful to the writers for allowing a glimpse of the passion he restrains to slip through. I mean passion in the widest sense, not just the sexual form, you understand. I'd like them to explore that a lot more throughout the next couple of years."

Teal'c: "I have heard of a place where people do battle... in a ring of jello."

Teal'c has certainly had his fair share of ups and downs. The first of the character's near-death experiences occurred after his old mate and god, Apophis, brainwashed him into thinking the humans were a bunch of infidels who had to be crushed once more. Luckily, Teal'c's other old friend and mentor was on hand to remove his Goa'uld symbiote, and let Teal'c decide which team to bat for. "'Threshold' was a pretty intense episode and a lot of fun to do," says Judge. "But they did have me almost naked in the snow, which I think was just a way of getting back at me for all the jokes I've played on people over the years," he moans.

With characteristic aplomb, Judge goes on, "Did you see that episode, though? I looked pretty fit, huh? I'd been working out all hiatus and even if I do say so myself, I think I was looking pretty good!"

Pretense

Carter and Teal'c keep an eye on developments.

Written by:
Kathryn Powers
Directed by:
David Warry-Smith

Guest cast:
Alexis Cruz (Skaara/Klorel), Frida Betrani (Lya), Marie Stillin (Travell), Garwin Sanford (Narim), Kevin Durand (Zipacna)

The Tollan, Narim, asks SG-1 to take part in a ceremony to determine which personality has control over Skaara. Taken as host by Klorel (Apophis's adopted son), the Goa'uld claims his is the dominant force. Whilst Daniel and O'Neill plead Daniel's brother-in-law's case, Sam and Teal'c realise that the Goa'uld chosen to speak for Klorel has an ulterior motive for being on the Tollan home world.

O'Neill: "The Tollan will guarantee your safety? Is that a 'money back if you're not completely alive' guarantee?"

HONEST TO A FAULT, executive producer Brad Wright admits, "I didn't really like it. It was a Kathryn Powers script that Jonathan re-wrote fairly heavily. Jonathan was always more keen on the story than I was, but that was because he was leaving at the end of season three, and he wanted to wrap up the Skaara/Klorel arc." Wright agrees that the decision of the show's co-creator made perfect sense: "It meant we could create new threats and new characters, but I never did like the device that allowed Skaara to talk freely. Also, I didn't like how Skaara just went happily back to Abydos after the Triad. It struck me that there would be far too much baggage." Wright feels that 'Pretense' was a very interesting psychological story: "It was almost the Picard story from *The Next Generation* where he returns after having been a Borg. Skaara had been a Goa'uld. He'd killed millions but — well — he just goes happily home." In defence, Jonathan Glassner offers, "Since Alexis Cruz was a semi-regular on another series, it was more difficult to bring him back and conclude that storyline, so we had to go with what we could get."

Wright does, however, feel the episode had some redeeming factors: "It was a way of meeting the Tollan again. I always liked them as a kind of bureaucratic balance. Through them we got to glimpse the kind of future that we on Earth would probably not want. They were the kinds of humans I hope we don't evolve into being."

Urgo

SG-1 returns from a seemingly routine mission with a fifth, unseen member. The fun-loving Urgo has implanted himself into the minds of SG-1, apparently to investigate and record new experiences. In exchange he provides them with the ability to function as one, and heightens their sensory perceptions. Unfortunately, SG-1's interaction with their invisible friend results in the group being relieved of duty and confined to barracks until a way can be found to remove the impish Urgo from their brains.

Written by: Tor Alexander Valenza
Directed by: Peter DeLuise

Guest cast: Dom DeLuise (Urgo/Togar), Nickolas Baric (SF Guard), Bill Nikolai (Technician)

Urgo: "I wanna live! I wanna experience the universe! And I wanna eat pie!"

WITHOUT A DOUBT, 'URGO' is a favourite amongst favourites. "We were all in hysterics the whole time," says Amanda Tapping. "Peter would start the cameras rolling and then yell, 'Hey, Dad! Just make up stuff at the end of the scene and make them laugh and... Action!'"

Brad Wright says that 'Urgo' is one that will stick in his mind forever. "Dom DeLuise had been a huge fan of *Stargate* since the beginning, and because we love his work so much we invited him to be in our show. Of course, we all decided that an episode would have to be written especially for him. Not that he took much notice of the lines! He'd just do his own thing, but it was hilarious."

Richard Dean Anderson remembers, "The most fun we had happened off camera, of course, but editing what was on camera became the biggest challenge because Dom is the most improvisational and spontaneous actor. The absolute joy of working on that episode was watching the father/son dynamic, with Peter trying to rein in his Dad enough to get the stuff that we needed." Anderson's only regret is, "We didn't have enough time to show all of the wonderful comedy that DeLuise is a genius at."

Peter DeLuise claims he simply couldn't rein his father in. "What I did do," he says, "was remind the writers that my father doesn't always stick to the written word. But the whole trick to making that work was that my dad's character was a free spirit, and therefore had lots of licence. He could be the cross characterisation of all four main characters. He could be the id — the pleasure centre of all four brains, so he had great licence to do what he wanted."

Urgo causes chaos.

A Hundred Days

Story by:
Victoria C. James
Teleplay by:
Brad Wright
Directed by:
David Warry-Smith

Guest Cast:
Michele Green (Laira), Julie Patzwald (Naytha), Gary Jones (Technician), Shane Meier (Garan), Marcel Maillard (Paynan)

When SG-1 have a starlit encounter with the magical 'fire rain' of Edora they realise that the inhabitants of a small village are in grave danger from falling debris from an asteroid belt. Breaking away from the main group to rescue the village leader's son, O'Neill is left stranded on the planet when a meteor strikes the Stargate site, burying it under tons of rubble. Earthside, Sam Carter works around the clock trying to find a way to retrieve their lost colleague.

O'Neill: "Teal'c! You are one stubborn son of a bitch!"

JONATHAN GLASSNER REVEALS SOMETHING telling about Brad Wright's writing background. "Brad used to write plays, and that's what gave him the writing bug," he reports. "Brad is really good at writing very dramatic episodes that don't need that much 'gung ho' action. You could produce many of them on stage."

Wright is very modest about his achievement. "'A Hundred Days' began as an idea our script coordinator, Victoria James, came up with about a planet which was bombarded by comets every few hundred years. It's one of those 'love it or hate it' episodes for most fans, and my own feeling falls somewhere in between. At the last Gatecon, several fans told me that O'Neill would never give up on going home, and that I was wrong to suggest he would go native after only three months."

From a fan's point of view, one of the mysteries remaining at the end of the episode was whether or not O'Neill had helped Laira get pregnant. Asked if he thought the Colonel would have returned to Earth under those circumstances, Richard Dean Anderson replies, "Well, if he knew — no! Of course not. For the story's sake and for the 'potential for intrigue' sake he was able to walk away — albeit somewhat sadly. But in real life I don't think he would have walked away at all." Smiling, he goes on, "As for what we might do with the story, now that everyone except O'Neill knows he might have impregnated a woman and have a child in another part of the galaxy — who knows? Stay tuned."

Laira and O'Neill – up close and personal.

Shades of Grey

O'Neill and Newman keep their eyes on the ball.

Jack O'Neill steals a weapon-disarming device during a diplomatic mission to Tollana. Unrepentant, he is forced to accept early retirement. Secretly joining forces with Colonel Maybourne and his cronies, O'Neill decides to 'take' whatever he feels is necessary rather than promote mutual trade or diplomacy. His last official request is that he be allowed to return to Edora to continue his relationship with the woman he left behind, but this trip through the Stargate hides a much darker purpose.

Written by: Jonathan Glassner
Directed by: Martin Wood

Guest cast: Tom McBeath (Colonel Harry Maybourne), Steve Makaj (Colonel Makepeace), Marie Stilling (Travell), Christian Bocher (Major Newman), Linnea Sharples (Lieutenant Clare Tobias)

O'Neill: "I'd rather be a thief and alive than honest and dead."

JONATHAN GLASSNER CREDITS RICHARD Dean Anderson with the idea for this episode: "Rick said he wanted to shake up O'Neill somehow, and explore his dark side. He actually wanted O'Neill to go really bad, but Brad and I realised that it might be irredeemable if our hero went completely off the rails. However, it did give me the idea of having the character fake that he'd gone bad, in order to flush out some really nasty characters."

Of Colonel Maybourne, Martin Wood says, "We've had some greasy characters but he is definitely one of the worst — or best, depending on how you look at it."

Wood remembers it was tough getting one particular idea in motion: "We wanted to create a revolving Stargate. There's a really cool shot where O'Neill walks through one gate and out of the other, and the idea I had (which everybody hates still) was that we follow O'Neill from the Earth Gateroom and go through with him to the off-world Gateroom (which was ours, covered in plastic), but look at it from outside the Stargate. We did it by panning along with him going past the Stargate, so essentially we split the Stargate in half. I felt that is what it should look like: there wouldn't be a time lag — O'Neill would just walk in one side and out through the other." Wood claims that when he suggested this he was shouted down with cries of, "Oh that can't happen!" "Unusually, Michael Greenburg was my strongest supporter. He's the one who actually said 'We're doing it,' so we did."

NEW GROUND

The Bedrosians have ways of making O'Neill talk.

Written by:
Heather E. Ash
Directed by:
Chris McMullin

Guest cast:
Richard Ian Cox (Nyan), Daryl Shuttleworth (Commander Rigar), Desiree Zuroski (Parcy), Jennifer Copping (Malin)

SG-1 are caught up in a war between the Optricans and the Bedrosians. Daniel, Carter and O'Neill are held captive by the leader of some hardline soldiers, whilst Teal'c is badly injured during an escape attempt, but is helped to safety by a young Bedrosian scientist. Teal'c must trust both Nyan's medical skill and willingness to learn if he is to facilitate SG-1's route off the planet.

O'Neill: "Hey Rigar! You know that 'we come in peace' business? Bite me!"

"I CONCEIVED THIS EPISODE thinking of evolution," says writer Heather Ash. "What if we went to a planet, a former Goa'uld colony, that believed in evolution... and they were wrong?" Ash goes on, "Brad Wright and Robert Cooper really helped get the action into the episode. Plus it was a great opportunity to see Teal'c in a new position, an utterly helpless warrior dependent on someone he didn't trust. Christopher Judge did a fantastic job."

Judge welcomed the opportunity to portray a rarely seen side of Teal'c: "So much of my character is based on the fact that anything that afflicts me is quickly healed by my symbiote, but here we tried something that was going to take a while. Many actors will play blind as helpless; I chose to show Teal'c dealing with the fact that all his other senses were sharpened. It was quite the challenge for me to act as though objects were flying all around me, because I don't think that flapping my arms at things that aren't there is something I excel at!"

Jonathan Glassner remembers the episode being a challenge for some of the actors. "They were kind of upset at having to sit in those cages forever!" Ash comments, "More bothersome was the large amount of dust in the air from the dirt shipped in to cover the floors of the tent." Amanda Tapping didn't mind this at all. She smirks, "The ones where I get totally, disgustingly filthy are the best!" Ash especially liked the realistic conclusion to the episode. "I loved that, at the end, we don't stick around and try to convince people of reality. We just get the hell outta Dodge."

Maternal Instinct

O'Neill surveys the Path to Enlightenment.

SG-1 become involved in a race against time to find a lost world and retrieve the child hidden by Daniel's wife, before Apophis discovers and absconds with the boy. Custodian of the combined knowledge of the Goa'uld, the child's wisdom could enable Apophis to rule over all the other System Lords. They scour the Stargate addresses till they come up with the planet most likely to be the legendary Kheb.

Written by:
Robert C. Cooper
Directed by:
Peter Woeste

Guest cast:
Tony Amendola (Bra'tac), Terry Chen (Monk), Aaron Douglas (Moac), Steve Bacic (Major Coburn), Carla Boudrea (Oma Desala)

The Monk: "Learn the path through the darkness into the next life."

"THIS IS THE FIRST of what I like to call the 'Glowing Alien Arc'," offers writer Robert Cooper. "When Sha're died, Daniel's purpose for being a part of the Stargate programme became a little cloudy. So we invented a quest to find and protect the Harsesis child."

Michael Shanks admits to being less of a spiritual being than Daniel Jackson but, ironically, the actor says he gets lots of poetry and books in the mail because "fans think I'm like Daniel and a wonderful, sensitive guy. But my girlfriend says, 'Yeah! But they don't know you.' I have to admit that I am a little bit more cynical about that type of path and though that's not necessarily for the better, that's just me."

Shanks enjoyed his relationship with the twin boys who played the Harsesis child: "That was a lovely experience. My daughter was just over a year old when we made the episode, so I was used to handling babies. We had a very limited time on set with the boys, but I just got comfortable with them and we managed to capture a couple of magic moments with them. The first is when Daniel first sees the baby in the chamber. I came up and just as the camera moved off me and on to the baby I made some sort of 'googoo gaga' face to him. The baby was looking up at me and his reaction was just so warm. The second was when I was about to hand the baby back to Oma Desala and he clung on to my shirt. Those are moments which would be very difficult to reproduce, but were wonderful to experience and capture on film."

Crystal Skull

Daniel and Nick investigate the source of their problems.

Story by: Michael Greenburg and Jarrad Paul
Teleplay by: Brad Wright
Directed by: Brad Turner

Guest cast: Jan Rubes (Nicholas Ballard), Jason Schombing (Robert Rothman), Dan Shea (Sergeant Siler), Russell Roberts (Psychiatrist), Jacquie Janzen (Nurse), Christopher Judge (Voice of Quetlzelcoatl)

Emissions given off by a crystal skull cause a phase shift rendering Jackson invisible to those on Earth. In desperation, SG-1 turn to Daniel's grandfather, Nicholas Ballard, once a scientist of some note, now a voluntary patient in an asylum. Nick is able to see and hear Daniel, and together they work out that Daniel must revisit the chamber where the skull was found and ask the 'giants' there for help.

Rothman: "Teleportation Device? What do you think?"
Siler: "I think you're going to get fired."

BASED ON AN IDEA broached by executive producer Michael Greenburg and his godson Jarrad Paul, Michael Shanks also contributed to this episode. "I had been trying to write a *Stargate* script based on a piece of mythology about a crystal skull," he recalls. The idea had been planted when the actor was given a book full of the mysteries of South America. "This book was so incredible," expounds Shanks, "because it points out the inconsistencies of modern archaeological known facts with actual unexplained discoveries and phenomena. Apparently these finds are not reported in mainstream venues because they go against contemporary archaeological beliefs and would ask questions that we can't answer at this time."

Shanks says, "I started to write a story for *Stargate* about the crystal skulls. At the same time, Michael and Paul pitched an idea where Rick's character goes on this journey of discovery. But Rick said, 'Nah! I did that in *MacGyver*. I don't want to do it again.' So Michael said to me, 'Take this outline and see if you can add to it.' I did, then Brad Wright put it all together. I don't think the end result was exactly as Michael or I had envisaged, but most of the concepts remained and my strongest ideas, those of Daniel's grandfather and the crystal skull, were retained. To me it was a great episode because I got to see it from a writer's point of view and it is really something to watch a figment of your imagination come to life on screen."

NEMESIS

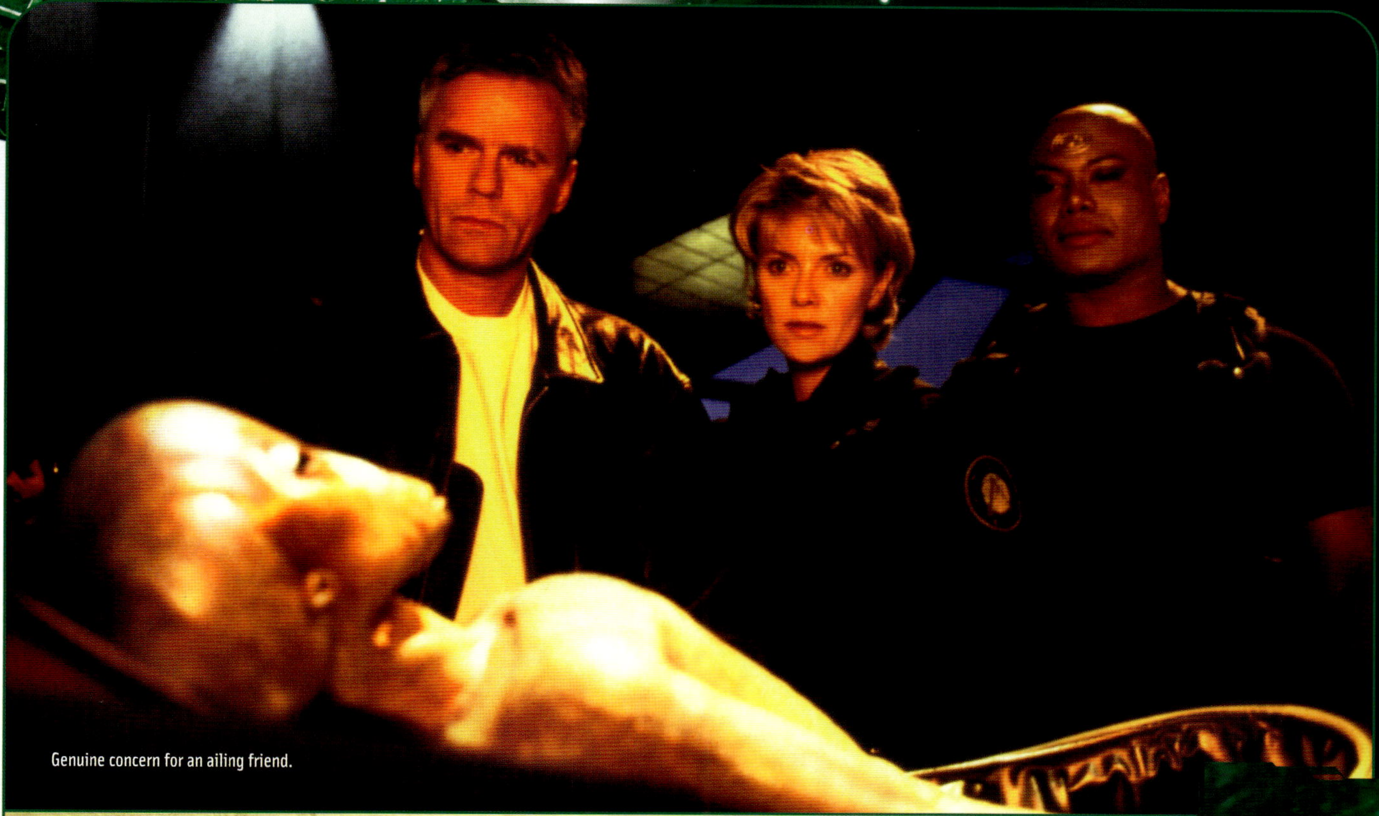

Genuine concern for an ailing friend.

Beamed aboard Thor's ship, O'Neill learns that the 'nasty technobugs' invading the Asgard vessel are in fact an even bigger threat to the universe than the Goa'uld. Thor insists the only way to stop the invasion is to destroy the ship before it reaches Earth's atmosphere. Prepared to die to save Mankind, O'Neill orders a massive amount of explosives to be transported on to the ship, and is less than thrilled when Carter and Teal'c arrive with them. The three use every skill they possess to try to save the day.

Written by: Robert C. Cooper
Directed by: Martin Wood

Guest Cast: Colin Cunningham (Major Davis), Gary Jones (Technician), Guyle Lee-Fraiser (Technician #2)

O'Neill: "Say something."
Teal'c: "One small step for Jaffa."
O'Neill: "Very nice."

"ALMOST EVERY YEAR I'VE directed the end of season episode and this was the first one that scared me," admits Martin Wood. "because suddenly there's these new critters — the Replicators." Affirming that he and visual effects producer James Tichenor share a desire to make any effect organic, Wood explains, "It's like when the Stargate opens... I don't cut to it every time because the characters see it every day." Wood aimed to create the same feeling with the new technobugs. "I wanted to make it look as though they were literally coming from anywhere, anytime. When O'Neill is walking through the halls of Thor's ship, and one actually had to touch him, I said it was because we had to know that they weren't going to kill him straight off."

The director explains that this view was borne out of his experiences in Africa: "We're so used to animals running away from us, but in Africa, I found that they walked towards you because they don't know what you are." Wood transferred this attitude to the Replicators. "These creatures don't know what humans are, so they're going to scuttle over to O'Neill. They don't know whether to be scared or angry. He's not mechanical; he's not what they are looking for, so they just feel him out and walk past. He's no threat."

Season Four

Regular Cast:

Richard Dean Anderson (Colonel Jack O'Neill)

Michael Shanks (Dr Daniel Jackson)

Amanda Tapping (Major Samantha Carter)

Christopher Judge (Teal'c)

Don S. Davis (General Hammond)

Teryl Rothery (Dr Janet Fraiser)

Small Victories

Machiavellian Meccano – a deadly Replicator.

Written by:
Robert C. Cooper
Directed by:
Martin Wood

Guest cast:
Colin Cunningham (Major Davis), Gary Jones (Technician), Dan Shea (Sergeant Siler), Yurij Kis (Yuri), Dmitry Chepovetsky (Boris)

The SG-1 makes a triumphant return to base thinking that the Earth has been saved from the Replicators. Sadly, one of the creatures survived and killed the entire crew of a Russian submarine. O'Neill thinks they should to tow the sub out to open waters and blast it with a nuclear missile. He is overruled, it's left to the Colonel, Teal'c and a small elite force to try to overcome the bugs by close combat.

O'Neill: "I'd be happy to debrief you all, after I've debriefed myself for a nice hot shower."

DIRECTOR MARTIN WOOD SAYS there are two things that will forever stick in his memory from the filming of this episode: Firstly, the location: filming took place in a real Russian submarine, Foxtrot class, called The Blackbird. "This thing was very small, very cramped and very malevolent," Wood laughs. "Russian engineers must have walked through the sub making sure that every possible danger was incorporated into its design. It was like — 'You can run here, so make sure there is a sharp point to catch on.'"

Ever in search of the perfect shot, Wood had someone climb inside the torpedo tube, just to tip water out onto the actors each time they opened the tube door! "I hadn't even thought about how scary that might be, until I had to get in and shoot something myself. The tube was like a steel coffin. I'm quite broad shouldered, so I was squeezed in tight, and then when Jim Menard [the director of photography] shut the door it went completely dark, completely silent, there was no air movement and they couldn't hear me. I was screaming for them to open the door but they couldn't hear a sound. Eventually Jim opens the door and I'm hanging out, hyperventilating — a wreck. Jim says to me, 'Are you claustrophobic?' and I gasped, 'I am now!' I thought Scott from visual effects was one of the bravest guys around. I was only in there for a few seconds, but he was in there for ten minutes. I'm proud to be able to say we belong to a very elite club of people who've been inside the torpedo tube of a Russian submarine."

THE OTHER SIDE

Alar holds the key to a world's destruction.

In return for humanitarian aid, the leader of the Eurondan people offers advanced technology that could help Earth fight the Goa'uld. All he asks in exchange is unlimited amounts of heavy water – the waste product from nuclear fission – a deal to which O'Neill quickly agrees. Jackson is the only member of SG-1 who suggests that the Eurondans might not be as trustworthy as they seem...

Written by:
Brad Wright
Directed by:
Peter DeLuise

Guest cast:
Rene Auberjonois (Alar), Anne Marie Loder (Farrell), Gary Jones (Technician Sergeant Davis), Dan Shea (Sergeant Siler), Stephen Park (Controller), Kyle Cassie (Eurondan soldier), Kris Keeler (Zombie Pilot Ollan)

Teal'c: "He is concealing something."
O'Neill: "Like what?"
Teal'c: "I am unsure. He is concealing it."

"WHAT I REALLY WANTED to do is explore what happened if the people we befriend end up being bad guys," explains Brad Wright. "and explain the philosophical question, 'Why don't our allies throw technology our way?' There is a rationale, and part of it lies in the fact that anyone who is willing to just give stuff probably isn't truly aware of its power from an ethical perspective." Wright says if he had to go back, he would have been a little less heavy handed, but concedes, "I wanted to peel the onion a little more slowly, but in forty minutes you can't really do justice to such a deep concept."

Wright loved the dynamic between O'Neill and Jackson here but admits to getting criticism from fans: "They thought I was trying to put a wedge between them, but all I was trying to do was embrace what I perceived as a nice capability between the two actors."

The writer is bothered by one choice Anderson made, which Wright feels made a difference to how the ending was viewed. "After he had deliberately closed the iris, knowing he was committing Alar to death, he was supposed to have said, 'This is where we came in.' So, O'Neill's justification was the Eurondans were an inch away from their own doom and then we bought them some time. My feeling is that the line would have helped to make the episode more symmetrical but, you know, writers are like that and actors aren't."

Upgrades

Go ahead make my day. O'Neill in confrontation mode.

Written by:
David Rich
Directed by:
Martin Wood

Guest cast:
Vanessa Angel (Anise/Freya), Dan Shea (Sergeant Siler), Kristina Copeland (Waitress), Frank Topol (Big Guy), Fraser Attcheson (Jaffa Commander)

Invited to test some mysterious devices the Tok'ra believe could prove valuable in the fight against the Goa'uld, the human members of SG-1 find themselves equipped with super-human physical abilities. Their enthusiasm for the new armbands wavers only slightly when they find they can't take them off. SG-1 decides to ignore standing orders and dash off to inflict as much damage as possible on Apophis's latest building project, before their energy – or snacks – run out.

Hammond: "I thought the devices were supposed to enhance them physically, not make them stupid."

BRAD WRIGHT CONFIDES THAT this episode started with writer David Rich suggesting armbands that gave SG-1 super powers: "It was a great concept; however, David's eventual script was so ambitious that it unfortunately came under the heading of 'unproduceable', so Robert Cooper jumped in and did a quick and I think fairly expert rewrite, embracing the humour angle."

Wright picks out one of his favourite scenes: "I love the fight in the bar," he grins. "Robert asked why I wanted one, to which I replied, 'Because it would be so cool!' He went through hoops to try to make that scene work, God bless him — and it did."

Director Martin Wood recalls the 'device' used to represent the force shield was a stroke of genius from director of photography Jim Menard. He and James Tichenor were ruminating on how to achieve the effect when Menard jokingly suggested a big sheet of cling film. "I thought it was a great idea," laughs Wood. "So we stretched some cling film across the hall. Then Jim ran at it — and it worked! When it came to shooting, Jim kept saying, 'It'll never work. It'll look stupid.' Of course when you see the cast hit this, their faces flatten out. If you watch O'Neill's nose, it's all squashed against the side." Richard Dean Anderson wasn't the least bit perturbed. "I smacked right into it," he grins. "I didn't care what I looked like."

Anise fails to notice as Shan'auc shares a smile with an old flame.

An old flame of Teal'c's appears through the wormhole, claiming she can enter into two-way communication with her symbiote and gather information about the Goa'uld. Shan'auc offers to share these secrets with the Tok'ra in exchange for a willing host for her symbiote. Teal'c is initially sceptical about her claims until she teaches him how to communicate with his own larvae. All seems to be going well for Shan'auc's blending until a literal snake in the grass puts an end to all her efforts.

Written by:
Katharyn Powers
Directed by:
Peter DeLuise

Guest cast:
Vanessa Angel (Anise/Freya), Musetta Vander (Shan'auc), Peter Wingfield (Tanith/Hebron), Gary Jones (Sergeant Davis), Ron Hadler (Cronus), Sean Millington (Ro'nak)

O'Neill: "This whole talking to two people in one body really sucks."

"'CROSSROADS' WAS A GREAT experience because we got to explore Teal'c's past," declares Peter DeLuise. "Teal'c really struck gold there because Musetta Vander, who played Shan'auc, is incredibly talented and beautiful. She was a hench-woman in *Wild Wild West* and was a bathing siren in *Oh Brother, Where Art Thou?* But a little known secret is she was also in the running to play the part of Anise."

DeLuise has an instinctive feel for difficult roles, "Anise had screeds of expositional dialogue that was so hard to pull off and make interesting. See, Amanda Tapping does that every week and makes it look easy, but every once in a while some poor actor will come on and have to do it. This didn't happen with Vanessa, but sometimes it can take up to seventeen takes to get through the crazy stuff."

Christopher Judge laughs, "I loved that episode because I got to kiss Musetta all the time." Hastily insisting that the actress is indeed a lovely lady and a consummate professional, Judge explains, "We had a really good connection, and we had this natural competitive thing going right from morning one in the make-up trailer." Judge confesses that the time he enjoyed the most was on the last day of filming when they did the candle scene. "It starts off as me berating her, but quickly turns into her confronting me. We actually spent half a day just shooting the juicy part of that."

Divide and Conquer

Anise shows her gratitude in age-old fashion.

Written by: Tor Alexander Valenza
Directed by: Martin Wood

Guest cast: Vanessa Angel (Anise/Freya), JR Bourne (Martouf/Lantash), Kirsten Robek (Lieutenant Astor), Andrew Jackson (Supreme High Councillor Per'sus), Phillip Mitchell (Major Graham), Roger Allford (The President)

The Tok'ra High Council and the SGC are left reeling when two members of an SG team are turned into Zatarcs (programmed assassins) by Goa'uld mind control technology. Hammond has no choice but to invite two of his most trusted veterans to undergo a perilous procedure in order to clear their names from the list.

O'Neill: "I didn't leave because I'd rather die myself than lose Carter."

"WHAT WAS FUNNY ABOUT 'Divide and Conquer'," offers director Martin Wood, "was that whole Jack and Sam thing. It started in 'Solitudes' where they were cuddling up for warmth. I loved the way they delivered that joke so much that I thought, 'We have to do this more often.' So, in 'Into the Fire', O'Neill goes and gets Carter, and she sits up and she's naked. Then in the hallway, when they have to hide and she's too close to him, it's like, 'Wow! I am not supposed to be feeling like this.'

"Eventually Brad and Robert decided they really had to get the 'more than colleagues' relationship out of the way. Amanda and Rick were also tired of skirting round that arc. A lot of the fans weren't too keen either, so we decided to knock it on the head.

"Rick and Amanda really loved playing that scene with the force field between them, because it's just not the sort of thing that happens on Earth. No human being, to my knowledge, has ever been forced to look at the person they love through a force field, knowing that one or both of them is facing imminent death. I just love the way they are nose-to-nose and can't touch each other. Anyway, we got the whole 'feelings' thing out of the way, and I think that it was necessary and long overdue."

Wood is also in complete agreement with the move to kill Martouf. "That was important, because great characters have to go sometimes, just so the audience knows we mean business when we tell these stories. The fans went wild and vilify me every time they see me!"

Window of Opportunity

Teal'c and O'Neill experience that Monday morning feeling again and again after a trip to another world goes disastrously wrong. The team head to the planet P4X639, and discover another human. Malikai tells Daniel that he and his companions must leave, but when Daniel declines his advice, Malikai knocks him out. O'Neill and Teal'c rush to help Daniel and are caught in a mysterious flash of light, only to find themselves back at SGC, ten hours earlier...

Written by:
Joseph Mallozzi and Paul Mullie
Directed by:
Peter DeLuise

Guest Cast:
Robin Mossley (Malikai), Dan Shea (Sergeant Siler), Daniel Bacon (Technician), Bill Nikolai (Technician), Cam Cronin (Door Airman)

Teal'c: "Colonel O'Neill is right. Events do seem to be repeating themselves."

WRITERS JOE MALLOZZI AND Paul Mullie confess they had a ball writing this episode, although Mallozzi insists, "It was extremely difficult to come up with something unique." Mullie adds, "We did think about pitching it seriously at one stage — but that notion didn't last long. Our background is in comedy writing. It was natural for us to resort to type."

Brad Wright admits, "I immediately thought that what we didn't want to do was a reprise of 'Cause and Effect', which is one of my favourite *Star Trek: The Next Generation* episodes. But Joe and Paul said, 'No! We don't want to rip off *Star Trek* — we want to rip off *Groundhog Day*!' I thought that was hilarious, and allowed them to go for it."

Wright confides, "Near the third day of shooting we knew we were going to be several minutes short. I suggested that we should write a scene where Daniel tells them they can do whatever they want, without any repercussions; hence the juggling, the golf and the kiss. We needed something to show that they are not listening to Daniel. Rick said, 'Hey, we could juggle. I can juggle, so can Chris,' so off they went."

Wright laughs, "The golf scene came from a desire to do a long drive competition through the Stargate. There's no way that could happen in a 'normal' episode without diminishing the Stargate, but every time I went golfing, I would think about it. I am so thankful to Joe and Paul for allowing me to realise my dream."

On P4X639, O'Neill means business... again.

Watergate

O'Neill and Teal'c prepare to skydive.

Written by: Robert C. Cooper
Directed by: Martin Wood

Guest Cast: Marina Sirtis (Dr Svetlana Markov), Tom McBeath (Colonel Maybourne), Gary Jones (Sergeant Davis), Darryl Scheelar (Co-pilot)

The team at Stargate Command get what is in effect a 'busy' signal that renders their Stargate unusable. SG-1 discover that the Russians have a Stargate too, hidden in a secret compound in the far north. But the iris is inexplicably jammed open, stopping the US Stargate from functioning. SG-1 joins an esteemed Russian scientist in an effort to reach the second Gate and close it down.

Teal'c: "This does not seem wise, O'Neill."
O'Neill: "I said it was easy. Not wise."

"ONE OF THE BEST things about 'Watergate' was the absolutely gorgeous location — an incredible power station," beams director Martin Wood. "We were shooting in the top part, and the next week Peter DeLuise shot in the bottom. He kept complaining to me that we got the good part — but the entire place was tremendous."

Wood also says the shots of everybody diving out of the plane were a blast to do. "We were on the ground when that happened, and they were diving onto these huge cushions. What tickles me is Rick Anderson is the only one who actually looks like he knows how to skydive."

Wood reveals that the producers were less than confident when he said he wanted to film the mini sub from the outside, underwater. "They said it would be too complicated and expensive, but I said, 'This'll be really cool. We build a tank and we shoot through that, so it's basically a fish tank in front of the camera.' We ended up with a tank filled with clear glycerine, with an Alka Seltzer in the bottom so that it bubbles up in front of us. We shot a lot of the show through that."

Wood says the very best thing about the episode was working with guest star Marina Sirtis, the British-born actress best known for her role as Troi in *Star Trek: The Next Generation*. "She has quite a cheeky sense of humour, so I wish I'd known she was a mad soccer fan when we were filming — I could have shown her a yellow card every time she answered me back!"

The First Ones

Is this really a friendly Unas?

Daniel and his former research assistant Dr Robert Rothman discover a primordial Goa'uld symbiote whilst excavating on planet P3X888. They are unable to share their discovery before a young Unas attacks the camp and kidnaps Daniel. A rescue attempt by SG-1 is hampered by the fact that the water surrounding the area is alive with Goa'uld symbiotes, all looking for a host.

Written by:
Peter DeLuise
Directed by:
Peter DeLuise

Guest cast:
Dion Johnstone (Chaka), Jason Schombing (Dr Robert Rothman), Vincent Hammond (Unas), Barry Levy (Major Hawkins), Steve Bacic (Major Coburn), Russell Ferrier (Captain Griff)

Teal'c: "Trust me, O'Neill."
O'Neill: "What if I'm not O'Neill?"
Teal'c: "Then I was not talking to you."

BRAD WRIGHT RECOUNTS, "PETER DeLuise and I were out looking at locations. Peter leant over and mumbled, 'Er... Brad... I have this idea, I thought it would be cool if we went back to the place where the original Unas came from.'" Wright says, "I agreed it would be a great backdrop for a story so I told him to go ahead and write it." The executive producer jokes that for someone usually noted for his enthusiasm, DeLuise took some persuading to put the notion down on paper. "Peter kept saying, 'No! No! I'm not a writer.' But I said, 'It's a great idea so maybe you are a writer.' Granted I rewrote the script fairly heavily, but at its core is Peter's script, and he did a very good job of directing it."

Wright goes on, "I loved that episode, but it was inevitably risky, so it was one of those precious little personal successes that made me, as a producer, go 'Whoo! That one worked!'"

DeLuise is flattered that the episode is a firm favourite with fans, and to hear that one of the most appealing scenes is when Daniel shares the energy bar with Chaka. "I remembered how in the original movie Daniel gives the special candy bar to Kasuf, and Erick Avari holds it like a Turkish person would hold a cigarette, sniffs it, and finally takes a bite and goes, 'Bundie — bundie way.' I love that the fans like that scene; I hoped it would be something fans remembered."

Costume Design

Above: The original design sketch for Bra'tac's costume.

Christina McQuarrie: "Most of the people we clothe are misplaced humans from ancient cultures, which have evolved in a slightly different way. That's where we come in. We find the tricks to make them recognisable and give a flavour of that culture."

"I can't explain how I fell into becoming senior designer for *Stargate SG-1*," laughs Christine McQuarrie, "but I am very glad I did." Anyone who has ever marvelled at the variety, intricacy and sheer volume of the designs created by the lady would be more than happy to explain the reason for her appointment. From Egyptian goddesses to medieval villagers, McQuarrie and her team have consistently produced a breathtaking array of garments that put *Stargate SG-1* in a league of its own. Coming from a theatrical background, McQuarrie had been tempted into the costume departments of various high flying series, practising her art on numerous science fiction shows before being invited to work her magic on *Stargate SG-1*.

"I came on board pleading for them not to make me do aliens," she smiles, "not because I don't like aliens, but because my first love is period costume. I enjoy making and building things from scratch, and didn't feel I knew that much about the dress habits of weirder beings from other planets!" However, during the first two years, McQuarrie and her team wholeheartedly threw themselves into the learning process and came to love the idea of creating outfits for 'out of towners'. "It's not as stressful as I thought and can actually be a lot of fun," she points out. "Sometimes the aliens get created by our special effects department, but a lot of the time we just come up with an idea, and more often than not the writers will tell us to go ahead."

McQuarrie's first foray into the *Stargate* universe could have been terrifying for a lesser mortal, but her experience in manufacturing classic garments helped tremendously when it came to designing the original pieces for the show. The première episode, 'Children of the Gods', required around 200 costumes from different historical eras. "I used the *Stargate* film as a starting point, and then was inspired solely by visual interest," she explains. "By mixing modern fabrics with classic designs from Egypt, Rome, Assyria and the like, I was able to create costumes that gave a feeling of a particular society or time period without taking too many historical liberties. We didn't want the clothes to be too closely identified with any actual Earth culture, because they were meant to have been developed on different planets at different times. It wouldn't have worked had they been exactly like the clothes worn by our ancient Egyptians for example, but I did want to suggest the right kind of ambience."

Brad Wright: "I'm extremely proud of the way Christina McQuarrie and her crew continue to create a look that entirely compliments the sentiment of our episodes."

Above (left to right): Designs for Tanith (left), a Tollan Guard and the original costume design for Nirrti.

The process starts for the costume design crew very early on. "We get the script, read it and try to envisage what the writers would like. I'm not that great at drawing," insists McQuarrie, who claims she has to spend hours labouring over her own drawings whilst the production design art department sail through theirs. Her inspiration comes from all quarters: "I use reference books, paintings, sculpture, even the markings on a piece of driftwood can set me thinking!"

Believing that variety is the spice of life, the costume design team take elements from whichever culture is represented in the script and blend them in an unexpected way, often throwing in the odd element from an entirely different culture just to keep the overall look slightly off balance. The fact that the Stargate universe is made up of a motley collection of displaced persons helps this along. Says McQuarrie, "In the world and in real life, there are so many wonderful materials — wood, straw, plastic, metal — that can be used to augment any basic costume idea and turn it into something entirely wonderful. We combine modern man-made fabrics with designs we have taken from ancient Egyptian documents, for example, and end up with something that is totally appropriate for what we want to achieve."

SCORCHED EARTH

Written by:
Joseph Mallozzi and Paul Mullie
Directed by:
Martin Wood

Guest cast:
Brian Markinson (Lotan), Marilyn Norry (Hedrazar), Alessandro Juliani (Eliam), Rob Court (Caleb), Nikki Smook (Nikka)

SG-1 have managed to transplant an endangered community, the Enkarans, from a Goa'uld slave world to a new planet. But when a gigantic alien ship appears, bent on restructuring the surface of the planet to allow the race of dormant life forms aboard the ship to re-start their lives, the members of SG-1 must face up to a moral dilemma where it appears each member of the team has to go their own way.

O'Neill: "We're talking about a bunch of freeze-dried aliens here."

"'SCORCHED EARTH' WAS OUR first script and actually got us our job on *Stargate*," begins Joe Mallozzi. "Considering we come from a comedy base, this is quite a departure for us as it's a very serious, issue-driven piece where the members of SG-1 are forced to follow their own path as to where they stand on the moral dilemma." Mullie offers, "It comes down to a question of who has the right to live? The relatively small group of people transplanted there by SG-1, or the thousands of DNA samples ready to resurrect an entire civilisation?" The episode did pose some serious questions for everyone involved. Director Martin Wood comments, "We spent a lot of time discussing script points. Richard Dean Anderson, for instance, wasn't comfortable with the fact that O'Neill does things Richard did not believe in, and was reluctant to portray."

Careful viewers will see that when Daniel and the robot Lotan are wandering down a tree-lined avenue, they sneak the odd look back along the path. Martin Wood explains, "To everyone's total amazement a bear just came lumbering out of the woods as we started shooting. Most of us stayed pretty calm; we sent the grips out to coax it away, but our resident tough guy — Christopher Judge — who is a bit of an urban alien, took to his trailer and wouldn't come out! Michael and Brian, however, had to get on and do the scene. Hence the shifty looks backwards every now and then to see if the bear was back."

Sam and Daniel review the latest CD ROMs.

Beneath the Surface

Teal'c withstands the heat in the kitchen.

SG-1 are sent to work in the mines beneath the surface of an apparently ice-covered planet. O'Neill, Carter, Daniel and Teal'c are now called Jonah, Therra, Carlin and Tor, and are doomed to a mundane and miserable life as labourers. Unaware that General Hammond is trying to unravel the mystery of their disappearance, the four that were once SG-1 form a natural bond, pooling fragments of memory to rebuild a picture of their former lives and forge an escape plan.

Written by: Heather E. Ash
Directed by: Peter DeLuise

Guest cast: Alison Matthews (Brenna), Kim Hawthorne (Kegan), Laurie Murdock (Administrator Calder), Russell Ferrier (Major Griff)

O'Neill: "SG-1? What kind of a name is that for a team?"

PETER DELUISE MANAGED TO pull off his usual stroke of filling the scenes with big, sweaty guys and loads of dirt: "Yes, 'Beneath the Surface' was one of my successes there!" Asked whether the infamous 'Homer' line was scripted or an ad lib, the director replies, "It was definitely scripted, and because of the far reaching implications it was done in two different scenes. Whenever I speak to fans, it seems to me that they think all the funny bits are improvised by the actors. Because it's their faces that are on screen, they get the credit for a lot of the really good writing that goes on."

Paul Mullie and Joe Mallozzi smile, "We wrote the joke where O'Neill is describing a memory to Carter and he says, 'There's a man who's very important to me. He's bald and he wears a short-sleeved shirt. I think his name is Homer.' We actually wrote 'Homer Simpson' but Brad Wright thought it would be funnier if it was just Homer."

Amanda Tapping says, "We all love *The Simpsons*, Rick especially. Normally we try to get the laughter out during rehearsal, because when we start rolling film is being used and it's costing money. But Rick is the worst person on our crew for this — he'll turn and give you a little twinkle in his eye just before you start, and you're completely lost." DeLuise swears, "I love Rick's humour and his dry wit. It's a real thrill to work with someone like that and it's such a luxury to have it on a show that doesn't take itself too seriously."

Point of No Return

Written by:
Joseph Mallozzi and Paul Mullie
Directed by:
William Gereghty

Guest cast:
Willie Garson (Martin Lloyd), Robert Lewis (Dr Peter Tanner), Matthew Bennett (Ted), Mar Andersons (Bob), Francis Boyle (Sergeant Peters)

Hammond receives a taped message from one Martin Lloyd, who claims to have information on 'government conspiracies'. He's dismissed as a crackpot until he outlines details of the Stargate programme, so SG-1 goes undercover to investigate. First impressions would seem to indicate that Marty, who insists he's a displaced alien, is nothing more than a paranoid delusional. However, events reveal he may indeed have come from outer space...

Daniel Jackson: "I've never been on a stakeout before. Shouldn't we have doughnuts?"

JOSEPH MALLOZZI EXPLAINS, "THE idea for 'Point of No Return' grew out of the fact that there are lots of websites out there where the participants believe there is an actual Stargate programme, and that the show is a cover-up for what is really happening." Paul Mullie adds, "We went with the notion that our characters become involved with someone who thinks he knows the truth about the Stargate, and who turns out to be an alien who can only get home through the Gate."

Although Mallozzi feels the episode is interesting because the characters get out into the real world, he is relieved that he and Mullie managed to incorporate a Stargate: "We'd written a few episodes all of which took place on Earth and the producers eventually said to us, 'Guys, you do know the Stargate goes off-world, don't you?' We really wanted to stay with this show, so we kind of pandered to that thought," Mallozzi grins.

Richard Dean Anderson advises, "Working with Willie Garson [the actor perhaps now better known for his recurring role as Stanford Blatch in the series *Sex and the City*] is an experience everyone should have. Working with him is an absolute joy, and I wish he were a regular on the show so I could work with him all the time. He is one of the funniest human beings on the face of the planet and is wonderful just to be around, let alone work with. When we put him back in for our 100th episode [season five's hilarious 'Wormhole X-Treme!'] it made me very happy. I adore him."

Martin Lloyd points to an underground conspiracy.

O'Neill is very lost in space.

Teal'c and O'Neill show off the prowess of the X-301, an experimental craft created from the remains of a pair of captured Goa'uld Death Gliders. When the planned showcase flight goes awry, the two team mates go hurtling into outer space. It's up to Daniel, Carter and the Tok'ra to effect a rescue. Helplessly travelling further and further away from 'home', Teal'c and O'Neill must conserve every ounce of energy to have any chance of surviving their ordeal.

Written by: Michael Cassutt
Directed by: Peter DeLuise

Guest cast: Carmen Argenziano (Jacob Carter/Selmak), Colin Cunningham (Major Davis), Peter Williams (Apophis), Steven Williams (General Vidrine)

Jackson: "Well, we were kinda hoping you could, um, like, beam them out, or..."
Jacob Carter/Selmac: "Beam them out? What am I, Scotty?"

BRAD WRIGHT BEGINS, "THE goal was to do our version of *Apollo 13*. What I really loved, aside from the fabulous visual effects, was Richard Dean Anderson's embracing of the role of astronaut. If you look at his performance it's quite studied. The thing I love about Rick is that as irreverent as he can be when he plays O'Neill, when it's time to get serious he does so."

Peter DeLuise shares Wright's enthusiasm for both actors' performances: "The situation had plenty of potential to be boring — two guys sitting in a cockpit — they couldn't even see each other. I thought the way they played the two guys dying slowly was incredible. As they become more and more oxygen deprived, we see the subtleties of their characters, their layers, their vulnerability. When Teal'c compliments O'Neill for his friendship and O'Neill replies, 'Right back atcha', I don't think you could beat it for poignancy."

Brad Wright also mentions an interesting side note: "I thought it was hilarious that I got vilified by some fans who thought a person would explode if they were exposed to a vacuum. What was even more fun was that smarter and more informed fans came rushing to my defence by saying that what we wrote was technically more accurate. Now I'm not saying we don't bend the truth a little, but we do try to have some sense of specifics. It's cool that people recognise that."

Serpent's Venom

The torturer Terok in action.

Written by:
Peter DeLuise
Directed by:
Martin Wood

Guest cast:
Carmen Argenziano (Jacob Carter/ Selmak), Obi Ndefo (Rak'nor), Paul Koslo (Terok), Peter Williams (Apophis), Douglas H. Arthurs (Heru-ur), Art Kitching (Ma'kar)

During a mission to his home planet of Chulak, Teal'c is hauled off and tortured by minions of the System Lord Heru-ur. Unaware of his predicament, the rest of SG-1 teams up with Jacob Carter in an effort to stop an alliance between Apophis and Heru-ur. The team realise that the stakes are even higher when they find that the gift Heru-ur brings to seal the deal is none other than Teal'c.

O'Neill: "Do you understand any of that?"
Carter: "It's all Phoenician to me, sir."

CHRISTOPHER JUDGE RELATES, "MARTIN Wood directed 'Serpent's Venom' and he's always open to actors' suggestions. Now, I'm not really a method actor, but in this case I thought it would help my performance if I was actually in a state of discomfort. So those scenes where I'm hanging from the chains — I'm actually hanging by those little cuffs and, man, were they biting into me, but they helped me achieve what I was trying to show. Of course, I had to have lots of TLC afterwards to make up for my ordeal."

According to Judge, the actor Paul Koslo, who played Terok, the man sent to torture Teal'c, scared the hell out of everyone from the minute he turned up at the audition. "Martin told me when Paul did his audition scene, it was so fantastic that no one could tell if he was acting or if he was really crazy. Everyone was so freaked they sent Martin out afterwards to talk to him." Teasing that the producers were working on the basis that it 'takes one to know one', Judge hoots, "They sent Martin to decipher if the guy was really a nutcase or just capable of turning in a great performance!" Similarly, the actor's first meeting with the guest star caused a twinge of concern: "The first rehearsal was my first meeting with him and he came to set wholly in character and I went up to Martin and said, 'This dude's crazy!' That's when he told me the audition story. After rehearsal the guy and I talked and he turned out to be a very lovely man."

THE CURSE

The newly-awakened Osiris is not in a good mood.

Daniel Jackson discovers his former professor has been killed in a mysterious lab explosion. The professor was studying an ancient Egyptian jar which contained the preserved remains of a Goa'uld symbiote. Alarmed to find out that a second jar has gone missing and that a Goa'uld could be on the loose, Daniel enlists the help of Carter and Fraiser. Meanwhile, Teal'c accompanies O'Neill on a very challenging mission.

Written by:
Joseph Mallozzi and Paul Mullie
Directed by:
Andy Mikita

Guest cast:
Anna-Louise Plowman (Sarah Gardner), Ben Bass (Dr Steven Rayner), David Abbott (Dr David Jordan), Lorena Gale (Curator), Dan Shea (Sergeant Siler)

Teal'c: "We have caught nothing. We are fishing."

"I PLAYED A LOT of golf during that episode," confirms Christopher Judge. "Standing, watching O'Neill not catching any fish was not the highlight of the time I've spent on *Stargate SG-1*, but it was fun to play the humour thing to the full."

There was much humour off set too. Teryl Rothery giggles as she recalls the wardrobe requirements that inspired a new pair of alter egos: "I became Turtle to Amanda's Gazelle because I am fairly petite and was wearing this huge back-pack and this little baseball cap and Amanda said, 'Wow! You look just like a turtle.' Once we'd stopped laughing I asked her what animal she would represent and without missing a beat we both yelled out 'a gazelle' and it stuck. So now, not only do we joke about pretending to be Charlene and Minnie — two Southern belle beauty students — we are Turtle and Gazelle as well!"

Amanda Tapping says they were torn between laughter and screams as Michael Shanks drove them across the sand dunes that were meant to represent the Egyptian desert. "We were in an open jeep-type thing, and Michael drove like a bat out of hell. We were bouncing around and clinging on for dear life, not sure whether to laugh like banshees or scream like girlies. We were worried about rolling over but the safety guys just yelled, 'Just keep your arms in, you'll be fine.'" Happily, no actors were harmed in the making of this episode.

General Hammond

O'Neill on Hammond: "He's a very good, very bald man from Texas."

Don S. Davis is the embodiment of General George Hammond. Born and raised in the Missouri mountains, he remains a country boy at heart. When several injuries curtailed his football career in college, Davis stayed on to study theatre. Having spent three years in the army — "I was a captain during the Vietnam period," he says, "and though I was never stationed there I did serve in Korea. It was good experience for me" — Davis decided to return to his theatrical roots. He gained a Masters and a Doctorate in theatre studies and taught at Southern Illinois University. "The acting part came much later," he grins, "I was a late bloomer. I didn't take this up till I was in my forties." Ironically, he got his first break as stand-in for Dana Eclar, the actor who played MacGyver's boss. A veteran of over thirty films and television shows (including acclaimed performances in *Twin Peaks* and *The X-Files*), Davis is also an admired painter, sculptor and wood carver.

As the man responsible for keeping the Stargate Command Centre and the errant SG-1 under control, General George Hammond earns every penny of his commission. Not content to be the sort of officer who sits behind a desk blithely issuing orders, Hammond is there, watching, sometimes even standing by the Gate as his teams depart and, he hopes, return safely from their often perilous missions.

"There is a myth that officers in high positions can simply turn off their emotions and order their troops to do whatever it takes, even lay down their lives, in order to get the job done. That doesn't happen in real life," insists Davis. "I come from a military background. I was a captain in the US Army so have some inkling of what it is to be a soldier. Hammond is smart enough to know that when he sends them out and tells them to 'go save the world', his teams will try their best to do just that, but they won't necessarily do it by following his orders to the letter. What I try to bring to the character is a sense of care and compassion for the men and women under his command; trying to let them know that their personal welfare is uppermost in his mind, even when the stakes are high."

Davis is particularly happy to have been given a greater chance to show that side of Hammond's

HAMMOND

O'Neill: "There's a man who is very important to me. He's bald and wears a short sleeved shirt. I think his name is Homer."

personality throughout seasons three and four: "In 'Crystal Skull', Hammond finally got to express some fondness for Dr Jackson. There's a scene when Hammond has to tell one of his granddaughters — who incidentally are the lights of his life — that he can't attend a school event because he has to try to find a dear friend. Hammond has no idea that Daniel can hear him at the time, but I thought it was a wonderful way of showing the depth of feeling the General has for these people, even if he can't exactly wear his heart on his sleeve or show any kind of favouritism in the normal course of events."

That said, there have been several occasions when Hammond has gone that extra mile, often putting himself on the line for his top team. "'Into the Fire' was one example where Hammond committed a court-martial-able offence to get out there and try to save SG-1," Davis points out. "By leaving the base and stepping through the Stargate, he was directly defying his own standing orders, but he knew it was the right thing to do. One of the things I like most about Hammond is that whilst he's a by-the-book sort of man, he will think for himself and act accordingly."

Davis is proud to have been given the opportunity to portray such a commendable character. "The welfare of the men and women under his command has always been paramount in his mind. One of the things I hope I've been able to show is that here is a man who, when faced with a decision to send his people to places from where they might not return, will do it only when there is no other course of action for him to take." That said, Davis is also proud of the way the General knows when to step back, and hold fire: "There have been times when Hammond has had to reluctantly decide against military intervention, even for a rescue attempt, simply because it would mean putting yet more lives in danger. Every one of his people is precious to him but, sometimes, he has had to let go — always reluctantly, and always with regret. I hope I've been able to show that he has kept his integrity, without losing his humanity."

Davis has one wish for General Hammond in the future. "Everyone thinks of him as stern and straight laced — kind of fuddy-duddy really," he says. "What I'd like to see is an episode where Hammond becomes some alien's love slave!"

Don S. Davis sadly passed away in 2008.

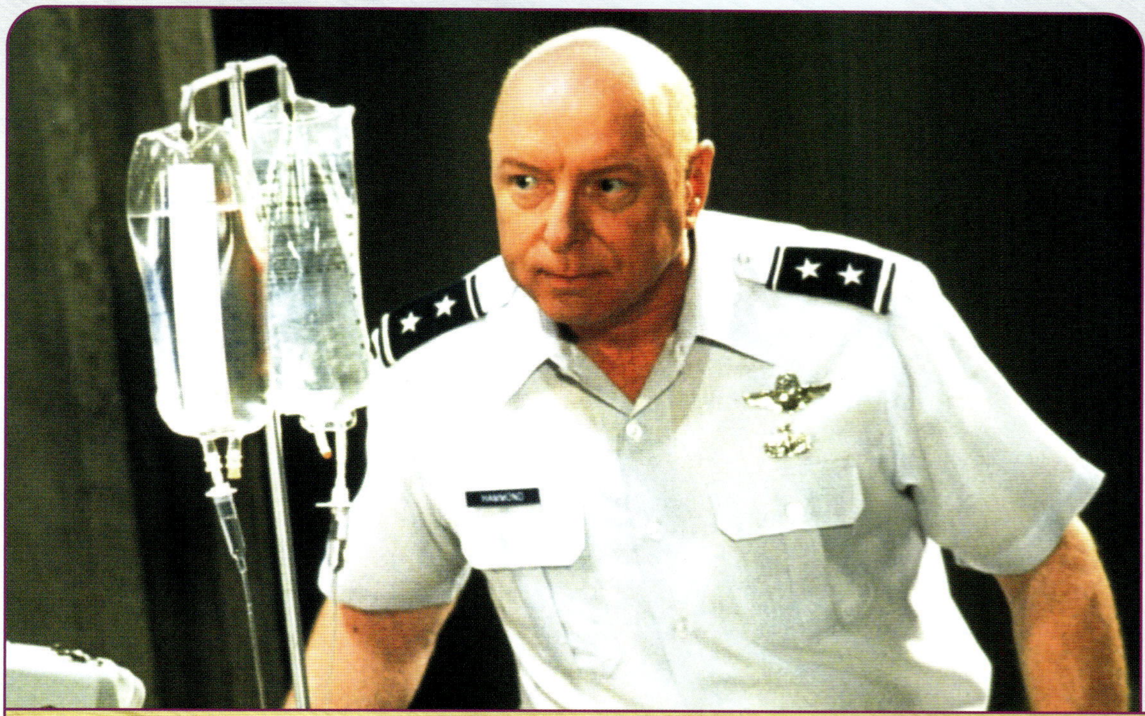

Thoughts on General Hammond

By DON S. DAVIS

I don't really know what to tell you about General Hammond other than he's a character that I enjoy playing. I think that as a young officer, he was a man who liked pushing himself to his limits, who enjoyed a bit of danger. It may be that that aspect of his character is what has made him so predisposed to overlook O'Neill's shenanigans. He admires Jack's courage, and his willingness to go to the limit in fighting for something he believes in.

The Air Force motto is 'integrity first, service before self and excellence in all we do'. One of the things I have tried to show throughout the filming of this series is that George Hammond is a man of great integrity, his word is his bond. He holds duty and honour in utmost regard. He is not going to betray his country or his troops if he can help it, no matter what. He may have to accept that, at times, people in his position in other divisions of the American armed forces might do things that are morally questionable or of questionable honour and integrity, but he doesn't like it. By nature he is a man who believes in doing the right thing at all times.

As for 'service before self', he actually resigned in one episode when his family was threatened because he couldn't compromise them, and he knew that he couldn't put himself and his family's interests above his duties and the needs of his country in command decisions. He felt he had no alternative, he couldn't betray his duty to his country, even for the welfare of his family.

And 'excellence in all we do'? Well, he expects his troops to do the best job they possibly can in any situation, and he tries to do the best job he can in every situation. He would be deeply offended by somebody in his command taking a slipshod or a lackadaisical attitude in performing their duties. He is a man who demands excellence from all of those whom he serves with.

I think Hammond loves his job. In the first episode he says to O'Neill, "I took this job so that I'd have an easy assignment that would allow me to look back over my career and work on my memoirs." Obviously he's had some kind of an exciting career or he wouldn't think that it warranted memoirs.

He's angry that Apophis came through the Stargate and attacked his base. He was initially angry with O'Neill, because he suspected that something about this man's initial reports was not true, or this wouldn't have happened. However, in the very first encounter, when O'Neill and his team go off, Hammond is shrewd enough to see that they are good people, and he dedicates himself to helping them get this job done for as long as it takes. I think he's a good guy. His wife has died, though he still wears his wedding band so he must have had a great love. He's got some grandkids that are the apple of his eye, he loves them so much that he is willing to step down rather than have them used as his Achilles heel.

CHAIN REACTION

Written by:
Joseph Mallozzi and Paul Mullie
Directed by:
Martin Wood

Guest cast:
Lawrence Dane (General Bauer), Tom McBeath (Colonel Maybourne), Ronny Cox (Senator Kinsey)

General Hammond announces that he is retiring. O'Neill protests that there is no way Hammond would do that voluntarily, but the General refuses to support the accusation and leaves his team in the hands General Bauer. Carter is immediately re-assigned and ordered to construct a planet-killing Naquadah bomb. Daniel and Teal'c are seriously demoted and demoralised. It's left to O'Neill to try to restore the status quo, but to do so he must seek assistance from a most unlikely ally.

Teal'c: "On Chulak, when a great warrior retires from the field of battle it is customary to sing a song of lament. Fortunately we are not on Chulak."

BRAD WRIGHT STATES, "'Chain Reaction' was a gem of a script by Paul Mullie and Joe Mallozzi, furthering the NID conspiracy storyline. It became obvious in season one that big epic adventures may be fan favourites, but with the limited budgets and time restrictions of television, we needed to create engaging storylines on Earth that had few visual effects or grandiose sets."

Don S. Davis feels 'Chain Reaction' allowed him to show the inner strength and moral commitment of Hammond: "One of the things I admire most about the character is that he knows how to play by the rules, but isn't afraid to question or stand up to them if need be. He is not the type of man to kowtow to anyone just because the rulebook says he should. As a dedicated military man, resigning from the United States Air Force was one of the hardest things he's had to do. However, the circumstances in which he found himself left Hammond no choice. He would not allow himself to become a pawn for a government agency that wanted to take over the SGC for some nefarious purpose and took the necessary but, in his mind, totally appropriate action."

If it looked as though 'Oscar' the dog was delighted to see Colonel O'Neill, it was quite possibly because, after his daughter Wylie of course, Zoe is the other girl in Richard Dean Anderson's life!

Right a bit, left a bit. Fire! Carter build s a Naquadah planet-killer.

2010

Teal'c, Sam and Daniel salute an absent friend.

It's ten years hence and Carter is married, Daniel Jackson is a well-respected scientist, Teal'c has lost his tattoo and O'Neill has gone fishing. A super race called the Aschen has taken Earth under its wing; providing the wherewithal to defeat not just the Goa'uld but life threatening diseases as well. But things are not as they seem, as the members of the former SG-1 realise the world is in grave danger, they must return to the past to safeguard the future.

Written by:
Brad Wright
Directed by:
Andy Mikita

Guest cast:
Christopher Cousins (Joe), Dion Luther (Mollem), Gary Jones (Sergeant Davis), Ronny Cox (President Kinsey)

Carter: "The Aschen can control planets. You don't think they can control the media?"

BRAD WRIGHT OFFERS, "'2010' is my favourite *Stargate*. It's my best work and though I write a lot of the stuff that doesn't have my name on it, you can be sure that if my name is on the writer credits it's going to be something that hasn't been done before, in episodic television at least." Wright was particularly pleased with the scenes between Sam and Joe, and Carter and O'Neill. "Amanda got nominated for a Gemini award for her performance in that episode, and I always take a little quiet pride when an actor gets nominated for something I wrote."

"That was a big episode for me," Amanda Tapping states. "I'm married to someone other than Jack, and I thought it was great that ten years on Carter has moved forward with a guy that is not O'Neill. And she is happily married, they are really in love with each other. I also loved the fact that I got to wear clothes other than army boots, that I was struggling with not being able to have children, and that there was still tension between O'Neill and me that seemed almost to be manifesting itself in hostility toward each other. I remember filming that scene where I'm at the cabin begging for his help. Originally it was written that he storms off and leaves me on his front lawn, but I said to the director that it made more sense for me to storm off, because I am the one who's moved on and who needs to leave again. So they let me do it, and I basically got to say, 'Well, fine. Have it your way. This is why I never married you, you stubborn little boy.' I loved that."

Absolute Power

Daniel ponders whether to have breakfast or destroy a chunk of the western world.

Written by:
Robert C. Cooper
Directed by:
Peter DeLuise

Guest Cast:
Lane Gates (Shifu), Peter Williams (Apophis), Colin Cunningham (Major Davis), Gary Jones (Sergeant Davis), William de Vry (Aldwin), Erick Avari (Kasuf), Steven Williams (General Vidrine)

SG-1 returns to Abydos and encounters a swirling sandstorm which twists itself out to reveal a young boy. Introducing himself as Shifu, the Harsesis, he allows Daniel to take him back to Stargate Command for tests. Shifu possesses all the knowledge of the Goa'uld and the boy decides to gift Daniel with all the genetic memories he holds. What Daniel chooses to do with such power is for him alone to decide...

Shifu: "Questions are plentiful. Answers are few."

ROBERT COOPER OFFERS, "Many of the stories I've written come from a personal desire to fill holes that I think develop from time to time in the series' ever-evolving mythology. I blame no one. Often it is me who has created the hole in the first place! We had often talked about 'all the knowledge of the Goa'uld' and about how it would help us defeat them. For once, I wanted to get a taste of what that knowledge was. The thing that attracted Brad and I to the story was the idea that the only form in which this knowledge could be had would corrupt us to the point of destruction. The Goa'uld seemed to be born evil. The genetic knowledge they inherit is so intertwined with awful memories that it cannot help but make them twisted. Only Oma Desala's power protected the Harsesis from its effects. It would be interesting to see what would happen to someone not so protected."

Many fans have wondered how lovely, sweet Daniel Jackson could turn nasty so quickly. Michael Shanks has the answer: "He never was a bad person; he was the same Daniel all the way through, we just saw him in a different set of circumstances. We all know that when Daniel is on the track of something he gets really passionate about it. This was Daniel being himself, and it was important to Robert Cooper and to me that we not tip the hand of what he was up to until the very end — that we perceive him as a bad person finally because we see the results of the process."

THE LIGHT

SG-1 discover what the Goa'uld do for pleasure.

Near death, Daniel Jackson returns from a mission to a remote off-world temple. One member of another SG unit has committed suicide, and two others are in a bad way. SG-1 visit the temple and discover a bright, mesmerising light that sends anyone within close range into a heightened state of euphoria, and also inflicts severe withdrawal symptoms on anyone attempting to leave the light's corona. The team's only hope of breaking away lies with a young boy found wandering around the abandoned site.

Written by:
James Phillips
Directed by:
Peter F. Woeste

Guest cast:
Kristian Ayre (Loran), Gary Jones (Sergeant Davis), Link Baker (Lieutenant Barber)

Daniel: "This thing isn't working."
O'Neill: "Did you check the batteries?"

ALTHOUGH MANY WOULD AGREE that Michael Shanks was totally convincing in this episode, Shanks himself takes a more pragmatic view: "It was one of those things where, when you do a character for a long time, particularly over four seasons, I had done so much with Daniel and played so many of those types of scenes that, to be honest, I was kind of over it. Just the previous season in 'Legacy' I had played a similar suicidal-type Daniel. In 'Need' the season before that, again he wanted to do something drastic and Jack had to talk him down. So with 'The Light', it was more of a challenge to try to find a different way to do that same kind of scene than it was to actually do the journey."

An actor who always analyses every facet of his performance, as Shanks puts it, "to the nth degree", he wishes he had had the time to do more with that particular scenario. "In 'Legacy' and 'Need' I had an entire episode where we watched Daniel unravel. In 'The Light' I think I had about the first ten minutes. Even though I had done it before I really didn't want to do it the same way, so it became one of those situations where I was whining to the producers: 'I've already done this. Why don't you get one of the other actors to do it?'" Shanks was eventually persuaded with the argument, "But you do it so well." However, he still maintains it was one of his bigger challenges.

PRODIGY

Carter and Cadet Hailey in accord, for once.

When Sam Carter meets Jennifer Hailey, she decides to take the cadet on a trip through the Stargate to give her a taste of what's to come should she rein in her temper. However, the routine mission to an off-world research base turns into a battle of life and death when a swarm of deadly life forms turn against SG-1 and the group of scientists they are protecting.

Story by:
Brad Wright, Joseph Mallozzi and Paul Mullie
Teleplay by:
Joseph Mallozzi and Paul Mullie
Directed by:
Peter DeLuise

Guest cast:
Elisabeth Rosen (Cadet Jennifer Hailey), Hrothgar Mathews (Dr Hamilton), Bill Dow (Dr Lee), General Ryan (Himself), Keith Martin Gordey (Professor Munroe), Michael Kopsa (General Kerrigan), Roger Haskett (Dr Bill Thompson)

Hailey: "Is it always like this?"
Carter: "Sometimes it gets quite exciting."

"'PRODIGY' STARTED WITH THE desire to show where the new recruits came from," begins Brad Wright. "But it was an attempt at starting a new thread that I probably won't continue with. I kind of wanted to create a new character, but sometimes these things just don't work out. I also thought it would be a fairly simple, under-patterned story. One of those cheaper episodes that we do to pay for the bigger ones, but those little glowing aliens — you would not believe how expensive they were!" Wright takes some solace in the set and the script: "Richard Hudolin did a fabulous job of the set, and that episode has some of my favourite jokes in it. The bit where Teal'c says, 'I am going to shoot you O'Neill' then floors him always makes me laugh."

Amanda Tapping says, "I think we fell short on the Carter/Hailey side. We had the potential to tell a story about the nature of genius and how volatile that is, and how you deal with it, but I don't think we explored that to the full." Tapping adds, "The premise of the Cadet Hailey arc was wonderful, though. It was a shame that we didn't have enough time to explore Hailey in more depth. If we had, we would have been able to see that her anger and frustration was borne out of having too much information in her head with no direction in which to really focus it. Elizabeth Rosen played Hailey with this edge, this stillness and that chip on her shoulder, which is ironic because in real life (and she won't mind me saying this) she is a real goof!"

ENTITY

When an innocent surveillance probe is perceived as a catastrophic threat, an alien race returns a more deadly device to infect the computers at the SGC. The entity escapes deletion by using the electrical circuit in the MALP room to survive and grow. Carter tries to communicate with it, but her attempt results in the entity growing ever stronger, now within Carter's own body. Hammond must decide whether to sacrifice one of his own in order to save the base.

Written by:
Peter DeLuise
Directed by:
Allan Lee

Guest cast:
Gary Jones (Sergeant Davis), Dan Shea (Sergeant Siler)

Hammond: "What on Earth is it?"
O'Neill: "Whatever has got into our computers has built a nest."

PETER DELUISE CAME UP with the idea for 'Entity' because, he thought, "It would be great to deal with the consequences of a 'consciousness in the machine' concept, but where the damage being done to our side was as a result of another race's self-preservation. We send out one of our routine probes but the very signal we're sending is hurting the aliens horribly so they return a death probe to stop us. I thought having the antagonist acting for some noble cause would make the story a little more interesting." Incidentally, DeLuise remarks that the electronic voice used by Carter was an homage to Amanda Tapping's hero, the real life scientist Professor Stephen Hawking.

Portraying a still, bed-ridden Carter was a major challenge for Amanda Tapping: "It was a really difficult episode for all sorts of reasons. First off it was so not Carter. This woman was so still and so angry and so dark. Considering I spent most of the time in bed, I was exhausted at the end of that episode."

Tapping continues, "I also found it quite hard to buy into the story, and these are the times when you just have to acquiesce to your character and say, 'OK. I'll just have to become Carter 110 percent and react to this situation as she would without analysing it as Amanda.' The beauty of it is having this great challenge of playing a very different Carter."

Carter, suffering from an overdose of alien technology.

DOUBLE JEOPARDY

Pride doth cometh before a fall. Cronus's finest hour.

Written by:
Robert C. Cooper
Directed by:
Michael Shanks

Guest cast:
Belinda Waymouth (Goa'uld officer), Jay Brazeau (Harlan), Ron Halder (Cronus), Matthew Harrison (Darian), Bill Croft (Sindar)

Daniel Jackson loses his head and Harlan returns to the SGC with a much subdued 'Comtrya' and a plea for SG-1 to go help 'themselves'. The robot SG team created by Harlan is trapped and tortured on an alien planet, and time is slipping away from both SG-1 teams who must fight to defeat the vengeful Cronus.

Harlan: "It's a very big emergency. You must help you."

ROBERT C. COOPER IS DELIGHTED with the way this turned out: "We had been trying to come up with a sequel to 'Tin Man' for a long time. We knew we wanted the robots out there doing what SG-1 did — exploring the galaxy. At one point, we thought we wanted SG-1 to have to save them from a difficult situation but the more we thought about it, the more we didn't know why SG-1 would get involved. Then we decided the robots had to help us solve a problem, and possibly give their lives in the process. That gave us the structure. Besides the great character of Harlan the robot, the thing that made 'Tin Man' interesting was the twist. You think you're following the real SG-1 and then you find out they're mechanical. I wanted to see if I could pull off the exact same twist again without making it feel cheap."

The episode was not without some challenges behind the camera. "Michael Shanks was supposed to get a nice easy episode to direct for his first time in the big chair," Cooper continues. "A scheduling nightmare made that impossible and we realised 'Double Jeopardy' was going to fall on his spot. It was one of the biggest shows we had ever attempted to produce. There was action, locations, huge sets and twinning [complicated VFX involving multiple characters played by the same actor in the same shot]. I think Michael thought it was my revenge for all those times he wouldn't say the lines I had written for him. It wasn't intentional. (Just an added bonus.) In the end, the episode turned out as good as it could have, and Michael did a solid job under difficult circumstances."

The ambush: will Teal'c survive?

SG-1 arrive at the home world of Vorash on Cronus's mothership with the intention of lending it to the Tok'ra long enough to facilitate a move to a safer planet. Tanith, a duplicitous high council member, lets Apophis know of the Tok'ra's intentions. The System Lord assembles his fleet and arrives at Vorash to wipe the planet off the face of the galaxy. SG-1's plan to use Apophis's arrogance against him goes awry, and the team once more finds itself adrift.

Written by:
Joseph Mallozzi and Paul Mullie
Directed by:
David Warry-Smith

Guest Cast:
Carmen Argenziano (Jacob Carter/Selmak), Peter Wingfield (Tanith), Peter Williams (Apophis), Malik McCall (First Guard), Kenton Reid (Red Jaffa), Paul Norman (Apophis's Red Guard)

O'Neill: "This is so the last time I help someone move."

ROBERT C. COOPER NOTES, "'EXODUS' was a real cliffhanger of a story in which SG-1 lend the Tok'ra their newly acquired mothership and get into trouble with Apophis's approaching fleet. It was truly massive on the visual effects side; we even blow up a star in this one! It also has a ton of space and space ship stuff which James Tichenor will tell you he dreads more than anything." Tichenor agrees it was challenge, saying, "It was pretty hard, but the results were the closest we've come to creating a really great space episode."

"Anyway," continues the executive producer, "Teal'c gets shot and is presumed dead. We always like to tease everyone, including the actors, as to who will be coming back the following season. Except Richard Dean Anderson, of course; it's hard to tease a guy whose name is above the title of the show."

Full of praise for the writers he says, "I know Joe and Paul wrangled with this script a bit, because the timing within the story was a bit tricky. How long does it take for a star to implode after you launch an open gate connected to a black hole into it? Need I say more? We also felt the need to service the Tanith storyline. We had built up this great rivalry between Tanith and Teal'c and then just dropped it for a long time. It's Teal'c's desire to make sure Tanith doesn't escape alive that drags O'Neill into trouble and ultimately gets Teal'c shot in the ambush." Is Teal'c really dead? And will the rest of SG-1 survive?

HAMMOND

SEASON FIVE

REGULAR CAST:

Richard Dean Anderson (Colonel Jack O'Neill)

Michael Shanks (Dr Daniel Jackson)

Amanda Tapping (Major Samantha Carter)

Christopher Judge (Teal'c)

Don S. Davis (General Hammond)

Teryl Rothery (Dr Janet Fraiser)

Teal'c returns to the Dark Side.

Story by: Brad Wright, Robert C. Cooper, Joseph Mallozzi and Paul Mullie
Teleplay by: Robert C. Cooper
Directed by: Martin Wood

Guest cast: Carmen Argenziano (Jacob/Selmak), Peter Williams (Apophis), Jennifer Calvert (Ren'al), Gary Jones (Sgt Davis), Thomas Milburn (Jaffa), Dean Moen (Jaffa)

The team find themselves stranded, along with Jacob Carter, hundreds of light years from home. Apophis is about to strike when another ship arrives, and attacks the Goa'uld. SG-1 board Apophis's apparently deserted ship, and quickly discover the reason for his hasty retreat – Replicators.

O'Neill: "He's looking a little pissed."
Carter: "We did just destroy his fleet."

"THIS IS THE EPISDOE where we end with Teal'c saying he's Apophis's boy!" director Martin Wood recalls. "The interesting thing in this one is that all of the ships you see are actually just one set. Apophis's Teltak, and the Peltak on the ship that we're in... and I'll explain the significance of that later...

"The main thing I remember is the hand-held running and gunning sequence. I had designed a shot: the idea was to run the camera straight at Rick, who was gonna start shooting. Then he spins around, and we see what he's shooting at, then we run with him straight at Michael. Then behind them, more bugs are coming, and they are shooting down at them. That was all done in one shot. When you see the finished episode, look for it, because it's spectacular! They ended up cutting away to the bugs on the wall, which I think was a mistake, because you can't see that the shot was all done in one."

The director reveals that the incendiary aspect of the weapons used in the show was very real: "The camera operator had to be decked out in body armour, because he was very close to these guns. So he was protected, but the walls of the set were made of Styrofoam, and the concussion from the shots actually moved the walls and created Styrofoam dust. As we're running you can see this white dust on the corner of the floor, and actually falling out of the walls as the Styrofoam grates against itself. It was hysterical!"

Teal'c and Drey'auc re-live fond memories.

A brainwashed Teal'c still believes himself to be the First Prime of his god. SG-1 call in Teal'c's former mentor Bra'tac, who decides that the only course of action is to deprive Teal'c of his symbiote and invoke the ancient 'Rite of Masuraan' – a ritual which allows Teal'c to re-live his painful past in the hope that he will once again see the truth and denounce his allegiance to Apophis .

Written by:
Brad Wright
Directed by:
Peter DeLuise

Guest cast:
Tony Amendola (Bra'tac), Brook Parker (Drey'auc), Peter Williams (Apophis), David Lovgern (Va'lar)

Daniel: "Did he just call me a woman?"
O'Neill: "I believe he did."
Daniel: "Obviously delirious."

TONY AMENDOLA SAYS 'THRESHOLD' is one of his favourite episodes: "Brad Wright developed the character, and really writes incredibly well for Bra'tac."

Displaying his knowledge of *Star Trek*, director Peter DeLuise begins, "We were in a little bit of trouble there at the start of season five, though we were a lot cleverer than the Voyager crew, because we managed to get back home in just one episode. We had to de-program Teal'c — all in forty-eight minutes! Brad Wright had the clever idea of bringing Teal'c close to death in the Rite of Masuraan." DeLuise continues, "We saw these wonderful — if I do say so myself — flashbacks of Teal'c when he was in the service of Apophis. We also see the wonderful Bra'tac in his former role as Apophis's First Prime."

Part of the episode was shot in hills above Vancouver — in the snow. "Chris Judge was a really good sport because he had to be topless," explains DeLuise. "He had been working out during the off-season and he was in prime fighting condition. He really put it all out there and kicked major butt." The director jokes, "We had a few cries of 'I'm freezing!' and 'I'm getting frostbite!' But we just ignored him."

DeLuise is also pleased with the flashback sequences. "You'll notice that it was very saturated with sort of a blue tinge to it, that was all director of photography Peter Woeste's idea, and I thought it was amazing."

ASCENSION

The things you can make with string, a piece of gum and a toaster...

Written by:
Robert C. Cooper
Directed by:
Martin Wood

Guest cast:
Sean Patrick Flannery (Orlin), John de Lancie (Colonel Frank Simmons), Ben Wilkinson (O'Brien), Eric Breker (Colonel Reynolds), Rob Fournier (Special Forces Commander)

The team find a planet apparently devastated by a Goa'uld attack. While investigating an alien weapon, Carter is rendered unconscious. Back on Earth she insists that she has been visited by Orlin, an alien whom no one else can see. Meanwhile SG-16 re-visit the planet in order to fire up the weapon. Orlin tells Carter that the weapon could spell disaster for the human race, and that the test firing must be stopped at all costs.

Carter: "So far he's only shown himself to me."
O'Neill: "Maybe he's shy."

"**I REALLY WANTED TO** do an old fashioned romantic comedy, but of course we had to add a sci-fi twist," writer Robert Cooper explains. "This is a sci-fi series after all! 'Ascension' gave us the chance to go home with the characters and see where they live. We were very lucky to get an actor of the calibre of Sean Patrick Flannery, who brought a completely unexpected level to the character of Orlin. Amanda won a well-deserved Leo award for her performance in this show. I think we fill her full of techno-babble so often that we forget she is a truly gifted actress, capable of really 'bringing the funny' when she's asked to. The scene with Teal'c and O'Neill at her door with the pizzas and videos is still one of my all-time favourites. Not just for the *Star Wars* reference and the cowboy hat, but Amanda's performance as she plays not only the discomfort at the prospect of having Orlin discovered, but the whole does-she-or-doesn't-she want O'Neill to think she has a man inside. It's great multi-level comedy acting."

For the 'Carter at home' segments Amanda Tapping notes, "This house was lovely and very Sam, but I wanted to add some really personal touches. The photos are my own. I've been given some lovely gifts by fans of the show over the years, so the quilts and the candles have been brought from home and are my way of thanking the fans for being so gracious."

The Fifth Man

SG-1 are under heavy fire from the Goa'uld during a mission to P7S441. Carter, Jackson and Teal'c return to Earth and tell Hammond that O'Neill is trapped, along with Lt Tyler. As no one back at the SGC has ever heard of Tyler, Hammond confines them to the base while they undergo medical tests. Carter hacks into the base computer, and discovers that the mainframe has been infiltrated and their personal files accessed.

Story by:
Joseph Mallozzi and Paul Mullie
Teleplay by:
Peter DeLuise

Guest cast:
Dion Johnstone (Lieutenant Tyler), Gary Jones (Sgt Davis), John de Lancie (Colonel Frank Simmons), Karen van Blankenstein (Nurse), Brad Kelly (Jaffa), Shawn Stewart (Jaffa), Dario Delaco (Jaffa)

O'Neill to Tyler: "I wasn't going to let you die, lieutenant. It's a ton of paperwork."

DIRECTOR PETER DELUISE BEGINS, "The alien was played by Dion Johnstone. Dion plays aliens for us a lot of the time, so it was kinda nice that we got to see his real face in this one." DeLuise continues, "He's Shakespearian-trained and was recently on stage here in Vancouver playing Tybalt in *Romeo and Juliet*."

DeLuise recounts his most vivid memory from the making of 'The Fifth Man': "We killed a lot of Jaffa. We killed too many Jaffa, apparently," he says. "At the end of the episode there is a shot of O'Neill and the rest of the guys, walking toward the Stargate. O'Neill had to walk around some of the dead Jaffas, and I got in trouble for showing that. I had to go to the 'How come?' room for that one! The Powers That Be said, 'Why did you have him step over that dead guy?' and I said, 'It's in the script! They took care of the guards. Where were they supposed to be? Gone? Missing?' It became this big issue — I was a bloodthirsty American director who liked dead bodies everywhere!" In the end they zoomed in on the shot of O'Neill stepping over the Jaffa, so that you couldn't see what he was stepping over."

Asked if there really is a 'How come?' room, DeLuise replies, "Of course! If the Powers That Be want to know 'How come you did this?' — you have to step into the 'How come?' room. They don't have a 'What were you thinking?' room on *Stargate*, because it would be too big. The 'How come?' room is a manageable size."

Three unhappy team members leave two behind enemy lines.

Red Sky

Three messengers of the gods arrive on Katal.

Written by:
Ron Wilkerson
Directed by:
Martin Wood

Guest cast:
Fred Applegate (Elrad), John Prosky (Malchus), Norman Armour (Dr MacLaren), Brian Jensen (Freyr)

SG-1 are welcomed as messengers of the gods on the planet Katal. But within moments of their arrival, the sky takes on an eerie red glow. A pre-recorded message from their god, Freyr, convinces the elders that this is indeed Ragnarok – the end of the world. SG-1 manage to establish direct contact with the Asgard but they seem unwilling to help save the inhabitants from destruction...

O'Neill: "What just happened?"
Carter: "Some sort of shift in the light frequency."
O'Neill: "Good – I thought I was having a stoke."

DIRECTOR MARTIN WOOD BEGINS, "They said, 'We're going to build this little town as an indoors set, because we want to have control over the colour of the sky.' That sounds weird, but the sky turns red in the episode, and we could change the lighting easily, because we were actually shooting the outside inside.

"There is one shot," Wood continues, "where we come out from behind a big tree and we hear the sound of a horse and wagon coming through, and you glimpse the wagon, and then you see SG-1 walking towards us. That was actually done by 'Evil' Kenny Gibbs and Dave Sinclair, the two props guys, pulling a wagon across the set. The rest of us were shouting, 'Faster you mules, get out of the shot!' It was all part of trying to convince people that we're outdoors."

Another memorable moment is the initial shot of coming through the Gate from SG-1's point of view, when they tumble down. "Originally the script said something like 'they come through the Gate, hard'," says Wood. "I said to the cameraman, Will Waring, 'I'm going to throw you through the Gate and you're gonna come up and land, shooting all the while.' He said, 'Do I have to?' but he went and got all padded up. He sort of tumbled through, holding a teeny tiny camera which made it look as though he were falling all over the place."

Rite of Passage

A dormant retrovirus, introduced by the Goa'uld Nirrti invades Cassandra's body, which starts to burn up under the strain. Nirrti is forced to give up her cloak of invisibility in order to retrieve a sample of Cassandra's blood, and is captured. She offers to help the child in return for her freedom. However, the System Lord has vastly underestimated the power of a mother protecting her child, and must battle Fraiser for supremacy over the young girl's health.

Story by:
Heather E. Ash
Directed by:
Peter DeLuise

Guest Cast:
Colleen Rennison (Cassandra), Jacqueline Samuda (Nirrti), Richard de Klerk (Dominic), Karen van Blankenstein (Nurse)

Hammond to Nirrti: "I should remind you that the woman holding the gun on you is Cassandra's mother."

ALTHOUGH KIDS DO CHANGE as they grow up, Cassandra underwent a complete change of body in this episode. Katie Stuart had originally played the character in the episode 'Singularity', way back in *Stargate*'s first season. Stuart was unavailable to reprise the role, so the producers returned to Colleen Rennison, the girl who admirably soaked Daniel Jackson in season two's 'Bane'. Peter DeLuise explains, "Everyone thought Colleen had done such a great job for us previously, and we were looking for a way to get her back. This was the perfect opportunity."

Teryl Rothery really relished the chance to show Janet Fraiser in a different light. "'Rite of Passage' will certainly be up there on the list of my Top Twenty favourite episodes," she declares. "It was just so much fun to make. We see another side to Janet, which I loved playing. I call it the 'momma bear syndrome'. You don't want to mess with this woman when it comes to her cub, Cassandra. Nirrti found that out the hard way! It was also the first time in five years we see that Janet does, in fact, have a home," the actress continues. "She doesn't live on the base after all. And in that home, she's not only dealing with a teenager with raging hormones, but a teenager from another planet that's been messed about by a Goa'uld. Whew!!"

Dr Fraiser takes care of her daughter.

Beast of Burden

SG-1 discover a planet where the Unas are cruelly exploited as beasts of burden.

Written by:
Peter DeLuise
Directed by:
Martin Wood

Guest Cast:
Larry Drake (Burrock), Dion Johnstone (Chaka), Alex Zahara (Shy One), Vince Hammond (Big One), Noel Callaghan (Boy)

Whilst conducting an anthropological study, Daniel sees his friend Chaka being captured by some men, and taken off through the Stargate. Following Chaka, SG-1 discover a race of people who keep the Unas as slaves, using them literally as beasts of burden. O'Neill and Daniel try to free the enslaved creatures, only to end up imprisoned themselves. Carter and Teal'c must come to the rescue...

O'Neill: "Where's Teal'c?"
Carter: "Trying to be popular."

"THIS WAS A REALLY cool episode," states writer Peter DeLuise. "SG-1 find themselves in this undesirable world of humans — who were controlled by a System Lord, and oppressed by the Unas. But once the System Lord left, the Unas's structure fell apart. The human 'slaves' then triumphed over the Unas and enslaved them in turn.

"This was my slavery allegory," DeLuise continues. "I really liked the episode because there's a big dilemma here: if we give the Unas a way of freeing themselves, it means a lot of people are going to get killed! We end up basically giving the Unas a way of defending themselves — but at what cost? Chaka, not being born into that sort of social order, immediately recognised that it wasn't cool to be imprisoned — so obviously he wanted to free his fellow Unas. This wasn't a very neat ending; it was very much a 'what have we done?' kind of a thing. In *Star Trek*, it's very clear: you don't go out to mess with a society — the Prime Directive states that you can't do that. On *Stargate* we break the Prime Directive every week! This particular case is a good example of where a prime directive might have helped us out." DeLuise feels 'Beast of Burden' shows *Stargate* at its best: "It doesn't bang you over the head with a message, but it still felt very strong to me. Brad Wright was my champion on this one. When I pitched a story about Unas slavery, he recognised its value straight away."

Daniel sheds some light on ancient text.

O'Neill is less than happy when he has to team up with a Russian SG unit to rescue a group of their colleagues who have gone missing off-world. Both teams investigate a Babylonian crypt where the bodies of the missing Russians are found. Whilst Marduk, a particularly unpleasant Goa'uld, stalks the unwary wanderers, O'Neill discovers the Russians have a secret agenda which threatens the lives of everyone.

Written by:
Joseph Mallozzi and Paul Mullie
Directed by:
Peter DeLuise

Guest cast:
Earl Pastko (Colonel Zukhov), Alexander Kalugin (Major Vallarin), Jennifer Halley (Lt Tolinev), Vitaliy Kravchenko (Lt Marchenko), Garry Chalk (Russian Colonel)

Daniel: "Yes, you go down the dark hallway alone and I'll wait here in the dark room alone."

PETER DELUISE EXPLAINS THAT, "'The Tomb' is the first time we feature a Russian SG-team on camera. Previously we had shied away from that, but now, based on our mutual Full Disclosure agreement, our lot had to integrate with them." According to DeLuise, co-producers "Joe Mallozzi and Paul Mullie came up with the idea, and it's basically the obligatory old horror movie set-up, where you're stuck with people you don't trust and there's something eating you alive. That's a great formula for some fun stuff! The set was amazing. We had hallways with tons of rocks and dirt. So, yes, it was a case of Peter DeLuise's dirty sets again!"

The episode was a particular favourite with Michael Greenburg: "It was shot by Peter Woeste and was one of our most visual shows. It had a great set and fantastic lighting — a lot of presence."

There was, however, a bit of a language barrier during filming. "We had real Russians, who spoke real Russian!" says DeLuise. "They also spoke English, but with incredibly thick accents. I'd find myself saying, 'Can you be a little less Russian?' I could see them looking at me, you know — 'What do you mean, less Russian? Who is this guy?' The trouble was in a Russian accent, the word 'colonel' comes out 'corn hole'. I'd be like, 'Please don't say corn hole, say colonel'. We can't have them saying Corn Hole O'Neill, because he's our hero. That was a source of great amusement, let me tell you!"

Dr. Janet Fraiser

Teal'c: "Dr Fraiser believes you are not strong enough to undertake such a mission."
O'Neill: "Yeah, whatever... " [thud].

Teryl Rothery is bright, bubbly and vivacious, totally unlike her SG-1 persona, Dr Janet Fraiser. "Brad and I had worked with Teryl on a number of occasions," says executive producer Jonathan Glassner, "and it didn't take a lot of thought on our part to sign her up." The actress couldn't be more thrilled that they did: "I went from a one episode guest appearance, to recurring, to regular cast member and thank my lucky stars daily for the privilege."

Within the precepts of *Stargate SG-1*, Dr Fraiser is cool, calm, collected and not the least bit scared of stepping into the fray. As Rothery puts it, remembering a particularly action-packed first season episode, "The girls kicked major butt in 'Hathor'!" Nor is Fraiser afraid of countermanding a higher-ranking officer. "She really did have the welfare of Colonel O'Neill, Sam and Teal'c as her main priority when she remonstrated with General Hammond in 'Fire and Water'," Rothery recalls.

Rothery is very pleased with the way her character has been allowed to develop over the past couple of years. "In seasons three and four we really get to reveal some of the facets that make Janet what she is, and get to see how some of the relationships have been nurtured and developed. One of my favourite episodes is 'Legacy', where SG-1 and I are infected by some alien technology unwittingly carried back to Earth by Daniel. I loved that we got to see Janet gradually lose control of her body and mind, and that she still fought so hard to find a cure. Usually she is the calm and collected one who keeps everything together. It was a treat to get to play her in such a vulnerable position."

Fraiser has been far more than a medic, particularly with regard to SG-1. "Although professionalism dictates that Janet gives her all for every patient she treats, I think it's fair to say she has a particularly soft spot for the guys in SG-1," Teryl Rothery says. "She raises a child with Sam Carter for a start, and is quite possibly the only person who can make Jack O'Neill lie still and take his medicine! Not that he does it for long, of course, but perhaps a millisecond more than he would do for anyone else... I think a great deal of love and respect has grown between the good doctor and SG-1 over the years."

Dr Janet Fraiser

By TERYL ROTHERY

She is the eldest of three children and has two brothers. Their names are Scott Jameson Fraiser and Jeffrey Sutton Fraiser. Her full name by the way is Janet Elizabeth Fraiser. Her father is a retired army officer, her mother a homemaker who would sew, do alterations and knit to bring in extra money. Not to mention keep her sane. Her parents' names are Jameson Franklin and Marjorie Kathryn Fraiser. Her mother's maiden name was Sutton.

Marjorie (although her friends and family call her 'Kate') is a very warm, fun-loving spirit. She has a wonderful sense of humour, which she has passed on to her children. Yes, as contained as Janet is, she does have a wicked sense of humour, you just don't get the chance to see it. There has been the odd occasion where you've been allowed to see snippets of it. I call her the iceberg because her core, her true essence is kept covered up. For the most part you only get to see what's on the surface.

The best thing that ever happened to her was Cassandra. Okay, it was the second best thing. The first was getting rid of that pompous, chauvinistic husband she was married to. Fortunately it only lasted three years. Three very long years!! Cassie has given her life balance. I really think having Cassie has allowed her to 'open up' somewhat. I think it's the first time Janet has really given herself permission to love.

Between Two Fires

O'Neill and Daniel in sombre mood at Omoc's memorial.

Written by:
Ron Wilkerson
Directed by:
Bill Gereghty

Guest cast:
Garwin Sanford (Narim), Marie Stillin (High Chancellor Travell), Peter Wingfield (Tanith), Gary Jones (Sgt Davis), Ryan Silverman (Tollan Guard)

SG-1 get an invitation to attend the memorial for Omoc, the Tollan. Narim tells them that before he died, Omoc was concerned that the Earth was in danger. The current High Chancellor offers to let Earth have access to Tollana's weapons of superior technology. The team discover that the hand of friendship has been extended as a trap to capture Teal'c and the rest of SG-1, and deliver them up to an old enemy.

Teal'c: "In order for the device to work on both of us, we must hold hands."

STARGATE SG-1'S CO-CREATOR BRAD Wright states: "I loved the moral dilemma here. Narim performs one of the most truly heroic acts we've ever shown on *Stargate*. People should also know that Rob Cooper did an excellent, and rather extensive rewrite of Ron Wilkerson's script."

For Amanda Tapping, 'Between Two Fires' was yet another episode where she loses a man. "Poor Narim," she says. Sighing about the fact that this unfortunate man did nothing to harm a soul she says, "I liked him, but I have to ask you to remind people that I did not blow him up! And I do feel pretty bad about the fact that Schrödinger (the cat) was on that planet when it blew up. Not only did I lose one of my boyfriends, I lost my pet too!

"I loved the joke where Narim had the computer with the Carter-like voice. I thought that was just hilarious." With another sigh, Tapping grins, "But I feel awful. I mean we just ran! We hauled ass! You could see the look on Narim's face: 'Go! Go! Save yourself!' and we were like 'OK, see ya!'"

Tapping adds, "Of course, as a mark of respect I do light a candle for my lost ones. In fact, my house doesn't need electricity any more because I light candles for all the men I've lost. I've got the brightest house in the street. When strangers turn up they say, 'What is she doing in there?' my neighbours say, 'She's lighting candles for all the men she's lost. There are thousands of them in there!'"

2001

SG-1 encounter the Aschen.

SG-1 encounter a potential new ally in the war against the Goa'uld. On the surface the Aschen seem to have it all – health, wealth and happiness. However, beneath the surface – deep underground in fact – Teal'c and Daniel discover the ruins of a huge deserted city. Daniel realises that the Aschen aren't quite the benevolent benefactors they portray themselves as. SG-1 have yet another battle on their hands.

Written by:
Brad Wright
Directed by:
Peter DeLuise

Guest cast:
Ronny Cox (Senator Kinsey), Christopher Cousins (Ambassador Joseph Faxon), Dion Luther (Mollem), Robert Moloney (Borren), Gary Jones (Sgt Norman Walter Davis), Howard Siegal (Keel), Rob Lee (Major Pierce)

O'Neill to Hammond: "These little chats of ours always bring me great joy."

THIS EPISODE IS THE sequel-cum-prequel to one of season four's standout stories, '2010'. Writer Brad Wright admits, "Like '2010', some of the locations were inspired by the available sets. Richard Hudolin, our production designer at the time, had designed a gorgeous and expensive set for 'Ascension' that didn't end up with much screen time, so it became the meeting room aboard the Harvester. And the underground city was rebuilt out of the town from 'Red Sky'. You'd never recognize either one, though!"

"We meet the Aschen again," Peter DeLuise offers, "but this time we meet them (and this is weird) in what may have been the original way we met them. Or is it an alternate way? We're not sure, but either tracks. In '2010', we saw that our future characters wrote a note to their past selves to let them know not to go to a particular planet. Here we see they had enough sense to follow that advice, but we still end up meeting the Aschen. '2001' shows us the alternate way of contact, where we met them via the third planet. I loved the way in which we were dealing with future knowledge wrapped in a cryptic package. I also loved that invention of Brad's — creating an entire world, as well as a whole new time. It's then we find out that Ronny Cox's character finally becomes President — that was kinda neat. And it was so cool that in this world, the Stargate has become the standard mode of transportation!"

Desperate Measures

Written by:
Joseph Mallozzi and Paul Mullie
Directed by:
Bill Gereghty

Guest cast:
John de Lancie (Colonel Frank Simmons), Tom McBeath (Colonel Harry Maybourne), Bill Marchant (Adrian Conrad), Andrew Johnston (Doctor), Ted Cole (Doctor), Carrie Genzei (Diana Mendez)

Carter is kidnapped and taken to a centre specialising in secret experiments. It transpires that Colonel Maybourne has sold a larval Goa'uld to an extremely rich and powerful individual, who wants to cure his terminal illness by becoming a host. The slippery customer first wants to find out how Carter managed to survive Jolinar's implant. O'Neill and Maybourne team up to track down Carter and the Goa'uld, unaware that the even slimier Colonel Simmons is working against their every move.

Daniel: "I think I just electrocuted myself."

WRITERS JOE MALLOZZI AND Paul Mullie are huge fans of the conspiracy storylines. Says Mullie, "I've said it in every interview, but I'll say it again: what I like, as a fan of *Stargate*, is variety. You can have a big arc-driven System Lord story; we can do a one-off comedic escapade. We also really need to have an NID facet. The episode is somewhat similar to 'Chain Reaction', in that we are looking into shady dealing of the NID." Joe Mallozzi continues, "Colonel Maybourne is fast becoming one of our favourite characters to write for. He's such a good bad guy. I mean, it's not like he's a Goa'uld, or has no redeeming qualities."

Actor Tom McBeath says, "I really don't remember that much about the show, other than I thought the writers did a pretty fine job. Plus I recall Richard sort of changed things on the fly in our scenes. I enjoy that. I love the dynamic we have together. We filmed part of 'Desperate Measures' in an old hospital for the mentally handicapped," McBeath continues. "It was full of ghosts, and was just a horrible place to be. The *Stargate* art department did a fantastic job with lots of on-set construction work, but even so, the place was probably built in the 1930s and at one time was presumably full of desperately unhappy people. There were stairways in this building with cages that were built to hold these people. It was really scary. I didn't see any ghosts, but you certainly got a very creepy feeling."

Carter encounters one slick, sick individual.

WORMHOLE X-TREME!

Four intrepid souls taking wormhole travel to extremes.

SG-1 are reunited with Marty the alien (last seen in 'Point of No Return', in season four). He is working on a new TV show which has a premise that owes rather a lot to the Stargate project. O'Neill is sent to the set to find out what is going on. Meanwhile, an alien ship has been detected en route to Earth, trying to connect with the pod Marty rediscovered on his previous encounter with SG-1.

Written by:
Brad Wright, Joseph Mallozzi and Paul Mullie
Teleplay by:
Joseph Mallozzi and Paul Mullie
Directed by:
Peter DeLuise

Guest cast:
Willie Garson (Martin Lloyd), Michael DeLuise (Nick Marlowe/Colonel Danning), Peter DeLuise (Director), Jill Teed (Yolanda Reese/Stacy Munroe), Robert Lewis (Dr Peter Tanner), Benjamin Ratner (Producer), Christian Bocher (Raymond Gunne/Dr Levant)

Dr Levant: "Just because they're aliens and their skulls are transparent doesn't meant they don't have rights."

IT'S A TOUCH OF the 'ET phones home' for this special 100th episode. Peter DeLuise says, "We tried to give the audience all the inside scoops that we could. If you watch the background, you'll see tons of visual gags and in-jokes. For example, Death Gliders being carried through the background; Thor, the puppet, being defibrillated — cool stuff like that." The director insists that a bit of poetic licence was taken with his own character. "As for the Pyrotechnics light show — I don't usually scream 'bigger, bigger!' but I do end up saying, in a calm, rational voice, 'This should be big. It should be fiery.'" Eventually he admits, "OK, it's Martin Wood's and my job to make things look big, so it's not totally unheard of for me to scream 'bigger, bigger, bigger!'

So what's DeLuise's favourite 'Easter Egg' in the episode? "The big crane shot at the end," he says. "That's our entire crew, the real one, onscreen right there. If you look really carefully, you can see the real O'Neill, and the photo double O'Neill. In the deep, deep background after the aliens go away in their ship, you can see that O'Neill and Teal'c are in the trucks almost at the top of the frame. But that is not really Richard Dean Anderson. That is, in fact, Bill Nicholai, his photo double. Richard is down towards the lower right portion of the frame in his civilian clothes, taking pictures!"

Proving Ground

O'Neill has a quiet word with the new recruits.

Written by:
Ron Wilkerson
Directed by:
Andy Mikita

Guest cast:
Courtney J. Stevens (Lt Elliot), Elisabeth Rosen (Jennifer Hailey), Grace Park (Satterfield), David Kopp (Grogan), Michael Kopsa (General Kerrigan)

A particularly promising group of academy graduates, which includes Cadet Hailey, get to shadow SG-1 in preparation for joining the elite at the SGC. When an unexpected 'foothold' situation occurs, it seems that Daniel Jackson has turned to the dark side, and O'Neill has been injured. The rookies are left to deal with this critical state of affairs on their own...

Carter: "Think back to when you were their age."
O'Neill: "I was never their age."

"THE EPISODE WAS QUITE funny because we just kept going from bluff to double bluff," begins Amanda Tapping. "It was like, 'Well, we have a foothold situation' and then, 'Naw! We were just kidding.' 'No Wait! We do have a foothold situation.' 'No, we don't!'"

Tapping relates, "I suddenly realised — I was around their age when I started doing this show. So I found myself reminding them of stuff because they would often forget things that are now second nature to the rest of us. For instance, how to carry your gun! In one scene, I am about to go into my lab, and I'm looking at the newbies — and they weren't flagging their triggers with their index fingers." Tapping explains, "You have to have your index finger straight next to the trigger of a gun, rather than curled around it, so that you don't just fire off accidentally. So, I'm standing off-camera going, 'Flag your fingers!' They were all going, 'What???' and I'm going, 'Never, ever have your fingers round the trigger. Look professional you guys, come on!'

"In another scene one of the newbies was holding his gun up ready, and I had to pass in front of him, but he kept it there. I just looked at him as if to say, 'What are you going to do? Shoot me? You lower your weapon when a friend walks past, and then bring it back up ready against the enemy.'" Tapping laughs, "I was getting stuck right in there! I remember thinking to myself, 'Wow! You are taking this just a bit too seriously.'"

48 Hours

SG-1 are staging a tactical retreat, but Teal'c delays his jump through the Gate to blow up Tanith's ship. The vessel crashes into the Gate just as Teal'c enters the wormhole, leaving Teal'c's essence floating in the ether. Daniel and Major Davis approach the Russians to request the use of their Gate, whilst O'Neill and Maybourne join forces again to rout out a Goa'uld in the hope that he could provide a way to release Teal'c.

Written by:
Robert C. Cooper
Directed by:
Peter Woeste

Guest cast:
David Hewlett (Dr McKay), John de Lancie (Colonel Frank Simmons), Tom McBeath (Colonel Harry Maybourne), Colin Cunningham (Major Davis), Bill Marchant (Goa'uld within Adrian Conrad), Garry Chalk (Russian Colonel), Gary Jones (Sgt Davis)

McKay: "I always had a real weakness for dumb blondes."
Carter: "Go suck a lemon."

"I STILL LIKE THE original title, 'Teal'c Interrupted', better," insists Robert Cooper. "I remembered an old episode of *M*A*S*H* where Hawkeye was trying desperately to get an incubator of some kind, I think. He had to continually trade one thing for another to finally get what he wanted. In that spirit, I wanted the team to have to face one obstacle after another before they are able to get one of their team members back.

"It actually turned into something very different to the M*A*S*H episode," Cooper admits, "with three completely separate yet intertwined storylines. I loved David Hewlett's performance so much, I wrote him a bigger part in 'Redemption'. By the way, the joke about McKay being allergic to lemons is a good-natured dig at a former writer on the show! I also thought we hadn't done a story that focused on the downright incredibleness of the Stargate in a while," Cooper points out. "Since it's our franchise, we should remind people every now and then how far out of our element we are when we try and use it!

"One last interesting tidbit is the death of Tanith. We would have much preferred to have him face off with Teal'c in a grand showdown, but the actor was holding us up and frankly we just couldn't afford to give him what he wanted. So the Tanith in the cockpit of the Alkesh is actually a computer generated effect!"

Teal'c prepares to dispatch Tanith.

VISUAL EFFECTS

Joel Goldsmith, composer:
"We have a terrific visual effects department. Often I try to imagine how grandiose and spectacular an effect will be and they always exceed my expectations and imagination."

Whenever you watch *Stargate SG-1* and hear a whiz or bang, witness an explosion or the mighty morphing military, spare a thought for the hard-working special visual effects teams beavering away with their pyrotechnics and computers blazing.

Innovative visual effects supervisor John Gajdecki is thrilled to have taken the opportunity to blow up the bad guys on this award-winning television show, although he took a bit of persuading at the start. "I had been working with the executive producers Brad Wright and Jonathan Glassner on *The Outer Limits*, but had decided to move on to pastures new," he remembers. "Brad and Jon kept phoning saying, 'C'mon we've got this great new thing going. Come on and do it!' However, I had other plans, which included going off and making movies, until I met one of the producers, Jeff King, at an awards ceremony. He reminded me that it was very rare to work on a show where everyone is your friend, so I decided to take a year out of my life and come work on *Stargate SG-1*. It turned out pretty well."

Above: The creation of the Asgard, Heimdall, was a special project for the visual effects team.

Opposite page: The Stargate 'Kawoosh'.

Gajdecki is president of GVFX, Canada's largest full-service visual effects company for the film and television industry. An amalgamation of multi-talented artists based in Toronto and Vancouver. Gajdecki was visual effects supervisor on seasons one and two of the show. James Tichenor worked as his assistant on the first season, then moved into full-time supervision and has since become the visual effects producer for the entire series.

The award-winning team of Gajdecki, Ted Rae and Robert Habros created the effects for the pilot episode 'Children of the Gods'. Tichenor explains how his colleagues designed the infamous 'Kawoosh' effect of the Stargate in operation. "It's such a dynamic turbulent effect it's almost impossible for us to build in CG," he reveals. "We have tried to do it a couple of times, because we wanted to have different camera angles and what have you, but it never turns out quite as realistic. What we actually did to shoot the 'Kawoosh' was prepare a tank of water, modelled on what they did to create the effect in the feature film, and blast it with a little air cannon. The high-powered air mover had a very focused nozzle exhorting major pounds per square inch of air

into a very, very small point. We set that up in the water tank, and used gravity to our benefit. We shot the air cannon down and placed the camera shooting straight up at 120 frames per second. So we got the effect of this funnel of water coming straight through.

"The whole shot took about three days to film," Tichenor continues. "Working in GVFX's model shop in Toronto, they knew exactly which angles they needed, took the camera down, made the environment as black as possible and just started shooting. They ended up with about ten different angles, which we still use to this day. Every time we need a 'Kawoosh' in an episode we refer back to the ones we shot almost five years ago. We composite them into new shots and always have to very carefully match the perspective angles, so it takes a bit of time to get right."

Michael Greenburg: "Our look just seems to be getting richer and bigger all the time with respect to SFX and VFX."

Below: The Goa'uld encounter an even greater evil, during 'Enemies'.

Tichenor is especially proud of the Emmy nominations they garnered for two very special episodes. "We try to do the best job we can every single show, but two episodes that are particularly dear to my heart have to be the season five opener and the closer, 'Enemies' and 'Revelations'," he smiles. "Those were the ones we got the Emmy nominations for.

"'Enemies' was big in that it had a real broad range of different effects, lots of virtual sets and then the granddaddy bugs, the soldier bugs and numerous versions of the Replicators. The episode was especially tricky because it was the third time we'd seen the Replicators, and we were continuing to up the ante in terms of what we could with them. We were trying to create more of a character for them. We also added newer bad guys into the mix, and then, of course, there was the final sequence, which was all shot with a hand-held camera, just because it made it look a lot more immediate, exciting and dramatic. Fortunately, those who watch the show thought the same."

Above: The Replicators roam through Apophis's ship in 'Enemies'.

Twenty-two weeks after shooting 'Enemies', Tichenor was just as enthusiastic about developing new concepts in visual effects: "'Revelations' at the end of the year was particularly special to us. For a year and a half, as a kind of side project, we'd been researching and developing a CG character based on the Asgard, Thor. Brad told me toward the end of the season that they were going to be doing an episode where we meet an Asgard scientist named Heimdall, who was Thor's buddy. We had got to a point where the testing with our CG character had succeeded well enough for me to go to Brad, and say, 'We want to try it out!'

"This character is kind of a Frankenstein creation," Tichenor reveals, further explaining how this very intricate little guy came to life. "It's actually made up of Teryl Rothery, who did the body performance and the voice (which, naturally, was digitally disguised) augmented by effects from Craig, the lead animator at Image Engine. All of the main body movements — arms and legs, body and torso — was motion capture of Teryl. The finer movements — the fingers, the hands and all the facial expressions — were done by hand by the animators at Image Engine. So while Heimdall doesn't actually look or speak like Teryl, he does move like her. So much so that, for instance, videotapes of Teryl performing the motion capture were used to help animate the Asgard's face.

"It's interesting," Tichenor continues, "because I see so many different people in that character. It's really weird how something that is not alive can look so real, like somebody who is actually standing there," he grins. "It's marvellous how that character worked; how everybody chipped in to make it turn out so well." With a modest shrug he nods, "So that was the end of season five for us. We made a promise to deliver a creature the like of which hadn't been seen before, and we did it! A lot of times, if the effects don't quite work, you can just edit around them or trim them down a little bit, but in this case we really had to deliver the goods. There was no other way, because Heimdall was the heart and soul of the episode." Laughing about the time and hard work it took to create some seemingly effortless scenes, Tichenor admits, "It felt great being able to do it... but we haven't been able to do it again since! It seems as though Martin Wood would like us to do motion picture-type extravaganzas every episode! It's true though, we just keep getting more and more ambitious. It's always intriguing trying to figure out where we'll go next..."

Summit

A gallery of rogues.

Written by:
Joseph Mallozzi and Paul Mullie
Directed by:
Martin Wood

Guest cast:
Carmen Argenziano (Carter/Selmak), Anna-Louise Plowman (Osiris), Cliff Simon (Ba'al), Courtney J. Stevens (Lt Elliot), Jennifer Calvert (Ren'al), Willian de Vry (Aldwin), Anthony Ulc (Major Mansfield), Vince Crestejo (Yu the Great)

SG-1, with the Tok'ra, embark on a bold plan to wipe out a shipload of System Lords. It seems that one powerful Goa'uld is attacking all the other System Lords. Naturally they all band together to decide what can be done with the interloper. Daniel Jackson agrees to go undercover as Yu's slave in order to deliver a poison which can kill all the Goa'uld present within seconds. However, the arrival of Osiris surprises Daniel and temporarily thwarts his plans...

Daniel: "It's kinda like Goa'uld Mardi Gras here."

DIRECTOR MARTIN WOODS FINDS that "the interesting thing about 'Summit' and 'Last Stand' is that they are two completely different stories, but most people don't realise that because there is a connection." A highlight for Wood was: "I liked that we got to bring in a new lot of System Lords, but the problem was some of them were played by extras, so only Ba'al and Olokum ended up with proper lines. Oh, and you get Bastet talking a little bit, but otherwise... zip. There was a lot of stuff cut out of 'Summit' in the end. We were eleven minutes over and it ended up being quite difficult shuffling stuff back and forth."

Wood has a particular soft spot for Ba'al: "Of course, we all love Ba'al. Cliff Simon has been back a number of times because he had a classic villain look. If he had a handlebar moustache he'd be twirling it all the time!" Co-producer and writer Joe Mallozzi was so impressed with the suave System Lord that he 'borrowed' Ba'al's costume from designer Christina McQuarrie's store to wear at the Gatecon convention in 2002!

Martin Wood adds, "'Summit' looked absolutely gorgeous. We had that beautiful set that allowed us to do that 'walk around' shot, where we introduced everybody. Christine McQuarrie really did us proud with those wonderful costumes. However, Michael Shanks hated his armbands; he thought they looked like water wings. I thought they looked great, but then again, I wasn't the one who had to wear them!"

Last Stand

Daniel sees to the petty needs of Yu.

Jacob Carter manages to convince a sceptical Daniel that Sarah can no longer be saved, now the Goa'uld Osiris inhabits her body. Daniel injects her with a mind-altering drug so that she believes him to be Yu's slave. Returning to the war council, Daniel discovers that Osiris is actually working on behalf of Lord Anubis. Things go from bad to worse when he also hears that Zipacna knows the location of the Tok'ra base, and has sent minions to destroy it...

Written by: Robert C. Cooper
Directed by: Martin Wood

Guest cast: Carmen Argenziano (Jacob/Selmak), Anna-Louise Plowman (Osiris), Cliff Simon (Ba'al), Courtney J. Stevens (Lt Elliot), Jennifer Calvert (Ren'al), William de Vry (Aldwin), Anthony Ulc (Major Mansfield), Vince Crestejo (Yu the Great)

Daniel: "You'd think a race advanced enough to fly around in space ships would be smart enough to have seatbelts."

MARTIN WOOD STATES, "IT was good to bring back Osiris: I loved the whole scene between her and Daniel where she walks in and just drawls, 'Daniel Jackson.' The changeover point was really interesting for me as director, because I didn't want them to do the 'Previously on Stargate SG-1... and now...' voiceover, I wanted to see the door closing and then the uninterrupted continuation."

Wood was also delighted by the visual effects. "We were in Tok'ra tunnels and there were huge explosions," he recalls. "James Tichenor barely has enough budget, but manages to put movie quality effects on the small screen. He's nothing less than a genius.

"Just look at that scene with the crashing cargo ship. Robert Cooper walked in and said, 'This is how I want it.' James and I were delighted, but went, 'It's going to be very expensive.' And Robert said, 'I don't care!' You get so conditioned to not getting that response in episodic television, so we really went for it. One of my favourite shots is when you see this glider going down, and cutting the trees. We shot it as a model, with blades on the wings. We also saw the inside of the cargo ship, which we shot by shaking the hell out of the camera! The end result would not have been so spectacular without Robert Cooper supporting us and pushing for that scene."

Fail Safe

In space, no one can hear you screaming to get out of a spacesuit.

Story by:
Joseph Mallozzi and Paul Mullie
Directed by:
Andy Mikita

Guest cast:
Colin Cunningham (Major Davis), Gary Jones (Sgt Davis), David Bloom (Spellman), Greg Anderson (Webber), Michael Teigen (Telescope Guy), Kristen Williamson (Jalen)

A giant asteroid is discovered hurtling towards Earth. SG-1 are sent to try to deflect the rock from its current trajectory, thus saving the planet yet again. However, the asteroid is in fact part of a huge plot by the Goa'uld, who have pumped it full of Naquadah so they can destroy the Earth without breaking the Asgard protected planet treaty. Can our boys and girls save us? It's time to suit up...

O'Neill: "Carter, I can see my house."

WRITER JOE MALLOZZI STARTS off by saying, "Every so often the fans will complain, 'This writer writes terrible scripts', but what some people don't realise is that we all have a hand in the scripts." Writing partner Paul Mullie butts in with, "Pay no attention. Joe is trying to weasel out of any responsibility for ripping off *Armaggeddon*." Obviously teasing his partner, Mullie goes on, "I don't think *Armaggeddon* was a particularly original idea in the first place. The concept of a giant asteroid crashing into Earth is a very old science fiction idea.

"What I always like to do when we do sci-fi stories that resemble films, or episodes of other shows, is to put the special *Stargate* spin on it — that little *Stargate* fourth act twist. In this case, it was the discovery that the asteroid was almost entirely made out of Naquadah. At first we thought we could just stick a nuclear bomb in it (that's what they always do in the movies), but then we realised — wait a minute, if we do that the result will be ten times worse!"

Mullie also reveals, "The real problem was the visual effects. We had to think of where the asteroid was in relation to Earth, and marry that to where the Earth was in relation to the ship, and where the ship was in relation to the asteroid! Sometimes you have to decide what is technically right, as opposed to what looks right, and vice versa. Joe was rolling his eyes, while Brad Wright and I were being two geeks having these long, involved discussions about the technicalities!"

THE WARRIOR

Master Bra'tac demonstrates the correct use of a staff.

Bra'tac and Teal'c encounter a charismatic Jaffa leader called K'tano, who has rallied a large group of Jaffa against the Goa'uld. SG-1 go to his base with supplies. O'Neill becomes suspicious when he hears that K'tano teaches the art of surrender rather than survival, and sends hundreds of people on suicide missions. Voicing his suspicions causes a rift between him and Teal'c, until it's discovered that the leader is in fact a Goa'uld masquerading as Jaffa.

Written by: Christopher Judge
Teleplay by: Peter DeLuise
Directed by: Peter DeLuise

Guest cast: Tony Amendola (Bra'tac), Rick Worthy (K'tano), Obi Ndefo (Rak'nor), Kirby Morrow (Tara'c), Vince Crestejo (Yu the Great)

O'Neill: "Hey, you in the skirt... get that target swinging a little."

PETER DELUISE EXPLAINS, "CHRIS Judge came up with the idea of using Imoteph, who was kind of the da Vinci of the Egyptians. He was heavily into architecture and medical advancements, and after his death was deified in Egyptian mythology. We thought he'd be a good guy to look at, and we came up with a new slant on how System Lords could get followers.

"That was the first episode where we used a special camera rig that I invented," DeLuise explains. "We call it the Revolva. We used it on the *Matrix*-style shot where we were going round and round the actors — I was very pleased with the results we got."

"My memories of 'The Warrior'," Tony Amendola says, "are of Peter DeLuise's energy during the shoot. Peter's ability to energise people — when he is trying to control a crowd of a hundred, and get exactly what he wants from everybody — is a wonder to behold. Sometimes he does it with a steady stream of profanity, which is hilarious. It's not offensive, and gets everybody pumped up and laughing because of what he's saying and how he's saying it." On a more serious note, Amendola shares, "I found the false messiah aspect of the story really, really interesting. Then came the realisation at the end where we say, 'You know what? We have to do it ourselves.' Ultimately, what it comes down to is the knowledge that you can't look outside yourself for answers. You really have to reach inside yourself."

MENACE

Written by:
James Tichenor
Teleplay by:
Peter DeLuise
Directed by:
Martin Wood

Guest cast:
Danielle Nicolet (Reese), Colin Lawrence (Major Warren), Tracy Westerholm (SF), Kski Gugushe (SF), Kyle Riefsnyder (SF), Dan Shea (Sgt Siler)

SG-1 encounter a young girl abandoned on a deserted planet. They discover that she is an android, with no memory of being manufactured. Daniel befriends the emotionally immature girl who presents him with a 'toy' in gratitude. Unfortunately, it's a gift that keeps on giving – with deadly results. Reese has been making Replicators which have destroyed the planet. Unable to deal with the magnitude of her mistake, the android goes quietly mad. Meanwhile, the Replicators attack.

Daniel: "It has a heart beat?"
O'Neill: "It has a heart?"

'MENACE' WAS VISUAL EFFECTS supervisor James Tichenor's first episode as a writer for *Stargate SG-1*. "I pitched a story where we go to a world and find a woman who has creatures she can control," he recalls. "We realise that she is actually an android, who uses these creatures as a defence mechanism. It's sort of a *Forbidden Planet*-type of thing. I'd pitched a couple of ideas in the past, but they had been laughed off (as well they should!). But this one caught the producers' interest. They thought, 'Hey... what if we make her the person who created the Replicators?' So they had me write an outline. Peter DeLuise then wrote a script, which Rob Cooper then re-wrote. The essence of my story is still there though. It all came from the idea that good people do bad things. I wanted to show that Reese, the creator of the Replicators, wasn't evil — just scared."

Michael Shanks comments: "'Menace' had a great emotional arc, coupled with the part of the mythology that deals with the origins of the Replicator technology. Personally, I enjoyed the little bit of Jack/Daniel tension. That was a highlight." Shanks also reveals: "My girlfriend Lexa Doig was originally asked if she would like to play the part of Reese, but she had commitments to *Andromeda* and couldn't do it. But working with Danielle was great. She's got a lot of 'chops', as we say in the acting world, and she did a wonderful job."

Carter and O'Neill are less than thrilled with Reese's toys.

The Sentinel

Gentle Marul, manhandled by menaces.

The dastardly Goa'uld are at it again, trying to barge in and take over a planet, but the indigenous inhabitants believe their super-shield Sentinel device will protect them. Unfortunately, the nerds at the NID have been up to their dirty tricks, and scuppered said device. Things look bleak until SG-1 enlist the help of two convicted criminals...

Written by: Ron Wilkerson
Directed by: Peter DeLuise

Guest cast: Henry Gibson (Marul), Frank Cassini (Colonel Sean Grieves), Christina Cox (Lt Kershaw), David Kopp (Lt Grogan), Gary Jones (Sgt Davis)

Kershaw: "I feel better just knowing there's an archaeologist watching our backs..."
Daniel: "... which end do the bullets go in again?"

A MAJOR HIGHLIGHT FOR the director of 'The Sentinel' was being in the presence of one of his heroes, a comic actor of the old school: "I got to work with Henry Gibson, who is wonderful." DeLuise goes on: "The original idea was to go and get some of our old bad guys to help us with this new mission. So we had these two characters which we implied were in the season three's 'Shades of Grey', in the crowd of personnel operating for the NID. In the 'Previously on Stargate...' bit, Brad Wright included a scene from 'Shades of Grey', but added in new shots of Grieves and Kershaw that we had in fact not seen 'previously' at all!"

DeLuise confesses that 'The Sentinel' will always stay in his memory because of the tragic events that unfolded during filming. "It was a challenge, because we were working on that show when 9/11 happened. We thought the whole world as we knew it was over, and here we were doing this silly sci-fi television show. A lot of film crews did stop filming, but we decided that whoever was trying to screw us up, did it because they wanted things to stop. We decided we were going to carry on working, as a way of saying, 'You didn't get to us.' We did that as a mark of respect for the people who died, and the families whose lives had to carry on. For me, it was very difficult to ask, 'Could you stand on this mark and say this line?' knowing that those buildings were crashing down and people were dying. It was one of the tougher days I've ever had."

Meridian

O'Neill finally admits his feelings for Jackson.

Story by:
Robert C. Cooper
Directed by:
Will Waring

Guest cast:
Corin Nemec (Jonas Quinn), Carmen Argenziano (Jacob/Selmak), Gary Jones (Sgt Davis), Mel Harris (Oma Desala), Dave Hurtubise (Tomis Leed), Kevin McCrae (Scientist)

Daniel appears through the Stargate suffering from high degree burns and a lethal dose of radiation. O'Neill tries to unravel the mysterious claim that his friend deliberately sabotaged an experiment on another planet. Meanwhile Daniel has to decide whether to return to this mortal coil or give it up to join the ranks of the Ascended, thereby continuing his spiritual journey.

O'Neill to Daniel: "I may have grown to admire you… a little… I think."

FROM THE MOMENT SPOILERS were posted online, enraged fans blasted the producers, the writing team, the suits at MGM and even the cast as having driven "poor Michael" out of the show. Some fans collected enough money to place an ad in a prominent Hollywood paper to show their solidarity for Michael Shanks. Though claiming victory for getting Shanks back in season seven, their highly vocal objections, simply underlined the massive amount of interest in the show.

There was much sadness on set during the actual filming of the episode. Teryl Rothery admits, "I was a wreck. I had some scenes where I just couldn't stop crying. Of course, it was ten times worse knowing that we really were saying *au revoir* to Michael too."

"I think that episode might stick in my memory!" Michael Shanks jokes. "Something happens to Daniel, and he packs his bags and moves on; he's no longer a regular character. That was kind of emotional. Everybody was saying goodbye to an everyday thing. I mean, these people become your family, and the ramifications of that never really dawn on you till afterwards. But I think I realised that what we had was coming to an end. There was a lot of emotional stuff on set, and it was difficult. I think the episode turned out well, considering the different agendas that were met. So, there's no discontent there, but what kind of closure can you achieve in any one episode? When all's said and done though, I think that for what it was meant to do, 'Meridian' was more than adequate, and serviced my character well."

Revelations

Osiris shows her displeasure at being thwarted by Thor.

Struggling without Daniel, SG-1 re-focus when Freyr, an Asgard buddy of Thor's, arrives and tells the team that not only are they in danger from the Replicators, but that Anubis has surrounded their planet and Thor has been taken prisoner and is presumed dead. The gang meet up with Heimdall, an Asgard scientist. Together they find Thor alive on Osiris's ship. O'Neill and Teal'c attempt to rescue him whilst Carter assists Heimdall to evacuate the contents of his lab.

Written by:
Joseph Mallozzi and Paul Mullie
Directed by:
Martin Wood

Guest Cast:
Anna Louise Plowman (Osiris), Teryl Rothery (Heimdall), David Palffy (Anubis)

Carter: "We were a team, Teal'c."

AMANDA TAPPING FEELS THAT this episode finally started to show how close Carter had come to all her team mates: "There's always been a sense of deep affection between Carter and O'Neill, but Chris Judge and I had been pushing for us to also see some tangible manifestation of Carter and Teal'c's relationship. I think we took some more steps towards that in 'Revelations', but we still have a long way to go." Tapping describes her approach to the episode: "Carter, O'Neill and Teal'c are still grieving the loss of Daniel Jackson. The way I play it is that my character has this need not only to talk about the loss of a very important person in our lives, but to acknowledge that we do feel this way and are having a hard time dealing with our feelings. It seemed to me that Teal'c and O'Neill were just a little too pragmatic. At first, I didn't think our concern came across that well, but having watched the episode again, there is a sense that the characters have their own private moments of grief over our loss of Daniel — but we do have to move on with our lives."

Richard Dean Anderson came under fire from some of the die-hard Daniel-ites after his comments about choosing to treat the archaeologist's demise in characteristically pragmatic terms. "But Jack O'Neill is a seasoned soldier," Anderson reasons. "He's seen action and has lost comrades. I think at this point in his life, it's reasonable to assume that he would take the time to grieve privately, but publicly he still has a job to do."